The fascination for details about the lives of servants was fuelled by the successful television series *Upstairs Downstairs* and is reflected by the interest visitors express in the 'below stairs' parts of country houses open to the public. This book documents the lives of the army of butlers, cooks, housemaids, gardeners and outdoor staff that made possible a life of elegant ease for those born above the salt.

About 1½ million domestic servants were at work in Britain in 1891, ranging from the hundreds employed by the largest houses to the solitary maid in an aspiring middle-class home in the suburbs. Domestic service thrived, obviously, because of the huge disparities in wealth, but also because it was at best a preferable occupation to many of the alternatives during the Victorian era.

Frank Victor Dawes gives a fascinating account, based on hundreds of personal reminiscences, of what it was like to serve in a large house or a modest suburban villa. He looks at the manifold duties, recruitment, wages, 'perks', living conditions, relationships with employers and high jinks amongst the lower end of the servant hierarchy.

'An excellent book ... serves as a reminder that the good old days were not so good for us.' Jean Marsh

'... this very readable history.' Ronald Blythe

'A fine account of nearly a century of English domestic service painstakingly researched and engagingly treated.' *The Times*

'Gives a thorough account of domestic service.' *Daily Telegraph*

Frank Victor Dawes worked from 1956 to 1960 as a reporter for provincial newspapers, then as Defence and Shipping correspondent of the *Daily Herald*. In 1972 he became a news editor and senior producer for BBC radio. His interest in the Victorian period and his mother's work 'in service' prompted him to write *Not In Front of the Servants* which became a bestseller when it was published in 1973.

Titles in the National Trust Classics series:

NOT IN FRONT OF THE SERVANTS

A True Portrait of Upstairs, Downstairs Life

FRANK VICTOR DAWES

CENTURY

LONDON SYDNEY AUCKLAND JOHANNESBURG
in association with The National Trust

First published in 1973 by Wayland

This edition first published in 1989 by Century, an imprint of
Random Century Ltd, in association with The National Trust for Places of
Historic Interest or Natural Beauty, 36 Queen Anne's Gate, London SW1H 9AS

Random Century Group Ltd, 20 Vauxhall Bridge Road, London SW1V 2SA

Random Century Australia (Pty) Ltd, 20 Alfred Street, Milsons Point, Sydney,
New South Wales 2061, Australia

Random Century New Zealand Ltd, 18 Poland Road, Glenfield,
Auckland 10, New Zealand

Random Century South Africa (Pty) Ltd, PO Box 337, Bergvlei 2012,
South Africa

Reprinted 1989, 1990, 1991, 1993

Cover illustration is a Pears' print *Christmas Comes But Once a Year!*

British Library Cataloguing in Publication Data

Dawes, Frank V. (Frank Victor), 1933 –
   Not in front of the servants: a true
   portrait of upstairs, downstairs life.
   [Rev. and expanded ed.]
   1. England. Domestic service, 1837 – 1950
   I. Title   II. Series
   640.'46'0942

   ISBN 0 – 7126 – 2981 – 5

Printed and bound in Great Britain by
Mackays of Chatham PLC, Chatham, Kent

Published in association with The National Trust, this series is devoted to
reprinting books on the artistic, architectural, social and cultural heritage of
Britain. The imprint covers building and monuments, arts and crafts, gardening
and landscape in a variety of literary forms, including histories, memoirs,
biographies and letters.

'Do not smile at droll stories told in your presence, or seem in any way to notice, or enter into, the family conversation, or the talk at table, or with visitors . . .'

(From *Rules for the Manners of Servants in Good Families*, 1901)

Contents

List of Illustrations

Between pages 128 and 129

Indoor staff and stable staff at Doxford Hall, near Ellingham, *c.* 1899 (Major A. S. C. Browne/Northumberland County Record Office)

Mary Webster, housekeeper at Erddig (National Trust)

Maid in a cap, photograph by Julia Margaret Cameron, 1860s (Royal Photographic Society)

Maids at Brandeston Hall, *c.* 1909 (Suffolk Photographic Survey, Ipswich)

Mr F. Pink, coachman to the Rawson family of Haugh End, Sowerby, from 1920 to 1925 (Calderdale Museums Service)

Gamekeeper at Erddig (National Trust)

Nurse, *c.* 1900 (Popperfoto)

Nursemaids and children in Kensington Gardens, 1913 (BBC Hulton Picture Library)

Nurse and baby on the beach at Southend (BBC Hulton Picture Library)

Queen Victoria at home with her lady's maid, 1896 (Popperfoto)

Victorian lady being dressed, 1865 (BBC Hulton Picture Library)

Preparing the evening meal at Burton House, near Petworth, *c.* 1895 (West Sussex Record Office)

The Finishing Touch, advertisement for Lemco, 1901 (Mansell Collection)

Superior Education (Mary Evans Picture Library)

A Black Indignity

A maid using a house telephone. Photograph taken for The Sterling Telephone & Electric Co. Ltd of London, 1912 (Public Record Office)

Parlourmaid preparing a bath before dinner, London, 1930s (Bill Brandt)

Another servant in the house this Christmas. Advertisement for the Western Electric Vacuum Sweeper, 1923 (Mary Evans Picture Library)

Preface

In April 1972 the *Daily Telegraph* published an appeal from me for the reminiscences of servants or employers of servants in domestic service in England. I was innocently abroad, on holiday with my family, expecting to receive at the most perhaps thirty or forty replies. Instead, when we returned home it was difficult to open the door for the pile of letters heaped on the mat.

There were two hundred and fifty of them and by the time they stopped arriving the total had climbed to over seven hundred. My young daughters were pressed into service helping to sort, sift and acknowledge them.

The majority, whether from servants or employers, were well written, factual yet evocative, nostalgic but surprisingly objective about the whole curious vanished order; some of them were funny but mostly they were sad. They provided a new perspective of a subject that was scarcely novel. For a century and more, English literature had been enlivened by haughty gentlemen's gentlemen – of the stamp of Jeeves and Crichton – Mademoiselle Hortense, the sinister French maid in *Bleak House*, and the down-trodden governesses of Charlotte Brontë's youth.

As early as 1861, when Mrs Beeton first published her *Book of Household Management* in collaboration with her husband, S. O. Beeton, it was being said over the teacups that servants no longer knew their place. Mrs Beeton took command and, in descending order from butler to wet nurse by way of footman, ladies' maid and nursemaid, gave them their orders for the day. She also offered a few words of advice for 'them upstairs':

The sensitive master and the kind mistress know that . . . with a proper amount of care in choosing servants, and treating them like reasonable beings, and making slight excuses for the shortcomings of human nature, they will, save in some exceptional case, be tolerably well served, and, in most instances, surround themselves with attached domestics.

Isabella Beeton was still in her twenties when she penned that magisterial statement, and she was destined to die before she reached thirty, yet she tackled the servant problem head on and left her mark on the structure of English middle-class domesticity. Like most Victorian monuments her *Book of Household Management* was built to last. The system and methods defined in its 1112 pages lasted beyond the reign of Queen Victoria, beyond the upheaval of the First World War and only fell into irreparable ruin in the years 1939–45.

It was during that period when bombs were falling on London that I first became aware of my mother's copy of Mrs Beeton's below-stairs bible, faithfully preserved from her own days 'in service'. What fascinated me in those days of ration books, when everyday delicacies such as ice-cream or bananas were unobtainable, were the mountains of jelly and raspberry cream depicted in the over-coloured plates which S. O. Beeton pioneered. They outdid even the Brobdingnagian mounds of mashed potato with sausages sticking out like the guns from a battleship turret with which the *Beano* titillated the tastebuds of its juvenile readers.

Mrs Beeton's descriptions of the duties of the housemaid et al were of no interest to me (as she herself majestically phrased it, 'We need hardly dwell on the boot-cleaning process.') There were no servants in *my* childhood. William Brown's family, in the *Just William* books, always had a housemaid, with frilly white cap and apron and black silk stockings, who treated our grubby schoolboy hero with disdain even though he was the son of the house. Up to 1939 no London suburban semidetached could consider itself properly middle class without a maid living in.

In the early 1970s, my friend James Render and I were discussing a suitable project for joint authorship. The subject of private domestic service came up. At that time the number of people employed in it in the United Kingdom had dwindled to fewer than one hundred thousand (not including au pairs) – a long way from the close on one and a half million employed in the latter years of Queen Victoria's reign, and as late as 1931.

What were the reasons, historic, economic, social, cultural and human, for this decline? *Below Stairs*, Margaret Powell's racy, light-hearted memoirs of her days as a kitchen maid, had aroused public interest, but my researches in the Reading Room at the British Museum uncovered little in the way of documentation or systematic study of domestic service.

So we decided to embark on a definitive social history. But no sooner was the project launched than James Render died at the early age of thirty-seven.

We had planned to spice the book with some human accounts to relieve the weight of statistics and social arguments. It was with this in mind that I sent off my letter to the editor of the *Daily Telegraph*. The replies flooded in from all parts of Britain and from overseas. Just a few came from people still employed in private domestic service, including one or two of that species thought to be extinct; there were still traditional English butlers happily buttling away in the shires.

My correspondents' memories of the past – tragic, comic, farcical, sometimes cruel – made *Not in Front of the Servants* an instant bestseller not only in Britain but in the United States as well. Jean Marsh, who played Rose in the highly popular television series 'Upstairs, Downstairs', wrote in *The Sunday Times*:

For me and other women of my sort, classless now but born well below the salt, [it] is not only an interesting record of what would have been our lot but serves as a reminder that the good old days were not so good for us. Nor perhaps for any woman, upstairs or down.

Others saw the significance of all this nostalgia somewhat differently. John Roche, one of President Johnson's aides, wrote in 1979:

Americans who have watched 'Upstairs, Downstairs' ... may have caught a number of significant tips on what ails Britain today. To put it in a sentence, the British never had a social revolution. Underneath that phlegmatic exterior the average Englishman or woman nourished a burning grievance against the 'bloody rich' ...

Roche went on to say that Americans visiting England as late as the 1940s were appalled at the way the British – one of the 'most class-ridden, inegalitarian nations in the West' – treated their servants as inanimate, invisible objects. Thirty years on, in the midst of what Roche described as 'an explosion of egalitarianism' in Britain, the former skivvies, poked fun at in countless forgotten drawing-room comedies of the nineteen twenties and thirties for being tongue-tied and malapropistic, had moved to the centre of the stage.

Servants were now taking the leading parts in television dramas and being interviewed for the colour supplements of the posher papers. The under-privileged slaveys who used to read pulp novelettes about aristocratic romance by candlelight in draughty attic bedrooms had become objects of compulsive interest to their betters. Relatives of peers wrote scholarly works about nannies.

What did the real life counterparts of Hudson and Mrs Bridges make of it all? We might never have known. Many of those who contributed their memories, experiences and reflections on which this book is largely based are sadly no longer with us. Their letters, which remain in the author's possession, constitute a unique archive, though some of them gave interviews on tape for documentary programmes broadcast by the BBC on Radio London and in 'Woman's Hour'.

It was James Render's wish that this book should be dedicated to the countless thousands, nay millions, of young girls and women who literally lived at the top and worked at the bottom, among whom I include my mother, who lived to the grand old age of ninety-two.

Frank Victor Dawes
August 1983

1
THE GREAT AGE OF SERVANTS

The days when butlers, footmen, cooks, nurses, governesses, housemaids and nannies were in plentiful supply are gone for ever. A servant class could not exist today because the whole order of domestic service in Britain depended for its survival on certain conditions which no longer apply. Domestic service thrived for two main reasons. First, because economic necessity forced larger poor families to put their children – meaning, mostly, their daughters – into service as one of the few means of feeding and clothing them, and putting a roof over their heads. Second, because servants 'knew their place' and accepted it as their lot in life to serve their betters.

In 1891, according to the Official Census, the servant class was among the largest groups of the working population: 1,386,167 females and 58,527 males were indoor servants in private homes out of a population of twenty-nine million in England and Wales. Of these, 107,167 girls and 6891 boys in service were aged between *ten* and fifteen years. These children were put to work from dawn until late at night for a few shillings a month and perhaps one half day off a week if they had considerate employers. They were required to wear uniform or livery, and their lives were regulated by strict rules. They slept in barely furnished attics and lived and worked in the dark lower regions of the big Victorian houses and stately homes. They had separate entrances (below ground), separate staircases (at the back of the house) and lives separate from those of their employers.

They were treated abominably by our present standards, not necessarily because they were cruelly treated but because for the most part they were regarded as inferior beings. Servants were used to seeing people laughing and talking and being agreeable to one another all around them, while at the same time ignoring *them* entirely. They were constantly the subject of jokes in *Punch* and other humorous journals in the 1890s. A favourite target was the supposed whimsical ways in which servants expressed themselves. For example: Cook to mistress: 'Oh, Mum, whatever shall I do for lunch? The butcher's been-and-gone-and-never-come!'

Punch was also quick to pounce on amusing examples of servants giving themselves airs, like the lady's maid who is giving notice:

Lady: 'Why, Parker? You came here only yesterday.'
Lady's Maid: 'I've been looking over your drawers, ma'am, and I find your things are not up to the mark and would not do me credit.'

Another *Punch* cartoon, under the heading 'Servantgalism,' satirizes the maid who objects to going to church on the grounds that 'in my last place I was never as'ed to go an' 'ear a curate preach'. Of course, parsons were just as likely to be held up to ridicule in cartoons as servants, but unlike servants they had an assured standing in society and could afford to ignore jibes. The fact that servants had sensibilities was rarely taken into account by the employers, who were used to treating them as people of minimal intelligence.

A cartoon by George du Maurier in 1877 depicts a lady telling her footman: 'You see this poor kitten the children have found? It is motherless. Get some milk Thomas! Mew like its mother! And feed it!' Employers simply did not realize how selfish they were in their relations with their servants; selfish, like spoiled children, from ignorance, or simply from the way they had been trained to look at things.

Whole armies of butlers, cooks and housemaids were employed in the great households of Victorian and Edwardian England, plus the battalions of grooms, coachmen and gardeners employed outdoors. At the turn of the twentieth century, the kitchen staff at the Duke of Portland's home at Welbeck Abbey comprised a steward, wine butler, under butler, groom of chambers, four royal footmen, two steward's room footmen, master of the servants' hall, two pageboys, head chef, second chef, head baker, second baker, head kitchen maid, two under kitchen maids, sundry vegetable maids and scullery maids, head stillroom maid, hall porter, two hallboys, kitchen porters and six odd-job men. The Duke also employed a head housekeeper, a valet, a personal maid for the

Duchess, his daughter's personal maid, head nursery governess, tutor, French governess, schoolroom footman and fourteen housemaids. There were six engineers and four firemen to look after the steam heating and the new-fangled electric plant, a telephone clerk and assistant, a telegrapher and three night-watchmen.

Outdoors there were more than thirty servants in the stables and a similar number employed in the newly installed garage, although it was more than a decade ahead of the time when the motor car would oust the horse-drawn carriage. Other servants worked in the gardens, home farm, gymnasium, golf course and laundry. Also, there was a head window cleaner and two assistant window cleaners.

The present Marquis of Bath lives in a converted mill-house just outside Warminster in Wiltshire, a few miles from the great house, Longleat, where he was born in 1905. The house is now open to the public and is famed for its private zoo and the lions that roam in the grounds. As a child, the Marquis had his own valet, one of forty-three indoor servants employed by his parents. Today he and his wife manage with just two resident servants, a married couple from Spain combining the duties of butler, footman, valet, cook and housekeeper, with 'daily' domestic help.

Lord Bath frankly admits to nostalgia for the 'good old days.' In an interview with the author in February, 1973, he said: 'I think the more servants one had the better. We had two lamp boys, two steward boys and about five footmen. You were looked after in the lap of luxury. If you ask me would I like to go back to those days, of course I would. Obviously one would, because it was much more comfortable for us, but I am not complaining because times have changed. It's so different from the old days when people were brought up to be in domestic service and they moved up from being lamp boys or pantry boys to footmen, groom of chambers or house stewards. It wasn't slavery exactly, but they were completely dominated by the hierarchy of the domestic servant class. Everyone, including us, was terrified of the housekeeper, Mrs Parker, dead a long time now I'm afraid. She would go around the house running her fingers along the tops of the shelves to see that they were dusted. The housemaids used to tremble.'

Servants in the great houses formed the aristocracy of domestic service. Most of those employed in the stately homes enjoyed comfortable standards of living and basked in the reflected glory of their high-born employers. But at the other end of the scale, no respectable villa in the suburbs was without its maid or maids, and the majority of those 'in service' in Britain were employed by the middle classes, not the aristocracy. These servants were mostly children, the maids of the kitchens, the tweeny or between-maid and the bootboys. They were mere chattels and slaves, whom their employers hardly ever saw, and frequently failed to recognize when they did.

True, a servant was paid a wage, although in the case of the lowest paid, a month's wages for a scullery maid in 1900 amounted to little more than ten shillings (50p), the cost of a good dinner at the best hotel in Brighton.

Also, unlike a slave, a servant was free to give notice and leave. But in practice, she or he was entirely dependent on the master for a 'character,' and without a satisfactory written reference from the previous employer a domestic servant stood no chance of finding another job.

A maid who became pregnant, perhaps from the amorous attentions of the eldest son or some friend of his visiting the house, could expect instant dismissal. It was unlikely her family would take her back, so she faced the workhouse or a life of prostitution.

The benevolent Victorians had a penchant for setting up voluntary organizations to help girls like these: the Metropolitan Association for Befriending Young Servants (M.A.B.Y.S.) and the Girls' Friendly Society are just two examples. But the law was heavily weighted on the side of the employers. It is surprising how few rights you had if you lived below stairs.

The Testaments were used to convince the servants that it was God's will that they should stay in their places at the bottom of society, and acknowledge the superiority of those they served. Texts and tracts were showered on the servants' hall and the words of John Keble were enlisted to the cause of subordination:

> The trivial round, the common task,
> Will furnish all we need to ask,
> Room to deny ourselves, a road
> To bring us daily nearer God.

Other oft-quoted texts were:

Servants, be obedient to them that are your masters according to the flesh, with fear and trembling, in singleness of your heart, as unto Christ; not with eyeservice, as men-pleasers; but as the servants of Christ, doing the will of God from the heart – Ephesians vi. 5,6.

Whatever thy hand findeth to do, do it with all thy might – Ecclesiastes ix. 10.

In their Highland retreat at Balmoral, Queen Victoria and her beloved Albert had started the practice of attending the neighbouring church at Crathie, accompanied by their servants as well as their numerous children. Victoria, who had solemnly stated as a small child: 'I will be good,' generated a national mood of self-conscious piety, the object of which was to 'do good' to children, animals, the 'poor blacks' and servants.

But 'love thy neighbour' did not mean treat him as an equal. The have-nots were after all part of the Divine order of things, to be saved from themselves with the Word and bowls of nourishing soup, but kept at arm's length. The barriers were maintained even in church. The middle classes, following the Royal example, took their servants to Sunday service with them, and nobody saw anything in the least questionable about the fact that the domestics were made to sit apart from their employers in separate pews, usually at the back of the church. On church parade the denizens of the basements were made to wear an outdoor uniform that made it clear to which class they belonged.

Yet many Victorians would have it that their servants were 'part of the family'. As Prince Albert movingly declared at an annual meeting of the Servants' Provident and Benevolent Society: 'Who would not feel the deepest interest in the welfare of their domestic servants? Whose heart would fail to sympathize with those who minister to us in sickness, receive us upon our first appearance in this world, and even extend their cares to our mortal remains – who lie under our roof, form our household and are part of the family?'

Household management books of the period, taking up the Royal cue, exhorted mistresses to look upon their servants as their children, to show a 'kind interest in their affairs' and make them rely on their own 'goodness and justice'.

Employers, as one might expect, did not always follow the rules. They could be kind and considerate or tyrannical and overbearing; they could be generous to a fault or incredibly mean. Some mistresses had the cutlery in the servants' hall stamped 'Stolen from . . .' and others were kinder to animals than servants, providing

19

better blankets for their cats and dogs than they provided for their maids. Mrs Lee of Somerton, Somerset, started in service in 1917 at the age of twelve. She was a kitchen maid to an elderly spinster who kept thirty cats. In a letter to the author she writes: 'My work consisted chiefly to cook for these animals and the amount of food cooked for them was wonderful – porridge for breakfast, a joint for dinner and a big saucepan of hot milk for tea.' In many houses servants were kept on short rations, either because the mistress was economizing or a dishonest cook was lining her own pocket. Ellen Russell writes from South Ealing of her own days as a tweeny in 1918: 'I usually bought myself a pennorth of broken biscuits, as I was always hungry.' Mrs Dorothy Shaw, of Newbury, who started as a tweeny in the previous year, says in a letter to the author that she once asked her mistress for a candle to light her attic bedroom. The lady cut a candle in half and gave one half to her with the remark: 'I don't encourage my maids to read in bed.' The usual ration was one candle a week for each servant.

Employers sometimes opened letters addressed to their servants to find out if they were keeping any secrets, 'tested' their diligence (and at the same time their honesty) by hiding coins under the carpets and in the loose covers, and locked out anyone who arrived back from an evening off so much as a minute late.

Some employers were eccentric to the point of being mentally unbalanced. In a letter to the author Mrs Pitt of Didcot recalls one mistress who was in the habit of touring the house in the small hours carrying a loaded revolver in a search for burglars. She would bang on the doors of the servants' quarters and on one occasion nearly shot the butler in mistake for an intruder. On another occasion she called the police and told them that her gold and diamond watch had been stolen. After all the servants had been hauled from their beds and questioned, the watch was found in the lady's bedroom. Mrs Pitt goes on: 'One by one the terrified staff left. One maid slipped away while Madam was at church, another didn't come back after her day off. Cook went on a visit and didn't return.'

Employers' fear of burglars was, however, understandable. As Kellow Chesney says in *The Victorian Underworld*, 'inside jobs' involving the servants were by no means uncommon. With streets full of beggars and pickpockets, the well-to-do felt constantly under threat, and fear followed them into their homes. House-holders and their servants were quite often armed with pistols or shotguns and it was not at all unusual for a butler or footman to sleep beside the silver safe in the pantry, with a loaded gun at hand. Some mistresses insisted on having the silver and other valuables placed at the foot of their beds at night, a practice that was usually regarded by their servants as mere eccentricity.

Victorian aristocrats were capable of eccentricity on a rather grander scale, however. The Duke of Portland had a skating rink installed in the grounds and if he came across a maid sweeping a corridor he ordered her out to skate, whether she had any desire to do so or not. The tenth Duke of Bedford detested women servants to such a degree that any who crossed his path after noon, when household duties were supposed to be over, were liable to instant dismissal. It was the rule in many great houses that housemaids must be virtually invisible above stairs.

In late Victorian days, Lord Salisbury was fond of riding a tricycle in the grounds at Hatfield House. He had a 'tiger' – a small boy in livery – to help him push it up the steeper slopes. On the way down this small boy had to jump up behind and ride with his hands on the great man's shoulders.

The third Lord Crewe enforced an inflexible rule at his Crewe Hall that no fires were to be lit except between 1 December and 1 May, whatever the weather might be.

Arbitrary rulings and commands of this sort hardly followed the divine rule of 'Doing unto others as you would they should do unto you' which so frequently appeared in the model housekeeping books of the time. While quoting the Bible, employers were as much concerned with the calm comforts of their homes (and the practical questions of who was going to carry the coal and empty the slops) as with the spiritual welfare of their servants.

Lady Bunting depicted the dreadful plight of a lady temporarily without servants in an article in the *Contemporary Review* of 1910: 'No one to cook the dinner, answer the door, attend to the children and carry out the many other requirements of an ordinary household. In many cases the mistress is absolutely incapable of taking on the duties which the servant has done and she finds herself more of a dependent than the servant. . . .'

When that moving description of upper-class hardship was written, more than one and a quarter million females were committing themselves to lives of unrewarding drudgery. Nearly forty thousand of them were less than fifteen years of age.

21

Yet even they were not as badly off as children who went into service half a century earlier. Elizabeth Simpson, born March 1853, was one of them. At the age of ten she was sent as a kitchen maid to a large house near Harrogate in Yorkshire. She had to get up at 4 a.m. to scrub the stone floors of the dairy with cold water and turn the butter churns until her little arms ached. For most of the year she rose in the dark and worked by the light of a single candle which she pushed ahead of her as she moved across the stone flags on her knees.

She was kept hard at work throughout the day, blackleading grates, lighting fires, polishing floors with the slops from the chambermaid's pail to make them shine, waiting upon other servants, until at 9 p.m. she crawled back to bed, again, for most of the year, by candlelight. It was a rule, strictly enforced, that she must never be seen by any of the family. If, by some mischance, they happened to meet, she must not speak to them, but curtsey and disappear as quickly as possible.*

Few, if any, of these children could read or write, so we have no way of knowing how they felt. We can only guess at the effect on a child of ten of being taken away from her family and put into this harsh environment. A letter written home by a maid in service at Edgware in 1870 is an all too rare example of a servant's thoughts:

My Dearest Mother,

I do not know how to thank you for your kindness in doing the aprons for me. I should never of got them made myself for I have not made the print dresses yet that I told you about when I was home last. I must try and finish them this week for I am sick and tired of seeing them about. I have been so driven at work since the fires begun I have had 'ardly any time for anything for myself. I am up at half past five and six every morning and do not go to bed till nearly twelve at night and I feel so tired sometimes I am obliged to have a good cry. I do think I should have been laid up if it was not for the Cod Liver Oil I am taking it is very nasty but I think it does me good it is very dear half a crown for a pint and it is so nasty. I reach my heart up nearly at the thought of it. Mrs Graves the cook is very kind. She as help me with my work in the morning. I would never of been done if she had not and these Nurse she as never said so much as are you not well not even offered to do a thing for me but I am much better now so I not trouble her. Dear Mother I should of ask you over next week only we are going to have two dinner parties one on Tuesday the other on Thursday

* Elizabeth Simpson was the maternal grandmother of Mrs Margery Bolton of Heysham, Lancashire, who, in a letter to the author, passed on this story, which she heard as a child.

and we shall be so busy so you must come after it is over. I have saved a small piece of plum pudding for you and will save some mince pies and I thought you would like a little dripping so I have sent all. Mrs Graves has to spare and I dearsay next week she will have some more. You must let me know if you would like it and I will send it. . . . Dear Mother I can give you plenty of mending when you have time and I should so like to see you but I cannot get away just now so you must come and see me soon. I let you know when to come for I have got lots of things to tell you. Dear Mother you have heard that poor William is dead and I know you did not like me writing to him but he was always very kind to me and it seems very hard for him poor fellow and he ill so long.

Hardly anyone to write to him or go and see him and he always very pleased to hear from me and he asked a friend of his to write to me as he was not able hisself. I do not know who this his that as been writing to me he comes from Sudbury Park very near to where William's mother lives. They wrote to me to go to the funeral but I could not go though I should very much of like to, he ask to see me just before he died. I hope dear Mother you will not be cross with me for writing this and when I see you I will tell you more which I have not time to write now hoping you are all quite well and baby better. With fondest love to all I remain your ever

Affect. daugher,

Harriet Brown

Please do write me a nice long letter one day this week excuse paper as it all I have. [Harriet Brown was the half sister of Mr Arthur Inch's mother. Mr Inch, a butler still in service, loaned this letter to the author.]

Twenty years after that letter was written, Harriet's daughter Ellen set off from her home in Bushey, Hertfordshire, to her first job in service, with a wicker box of clothes and a large label tied to her lapel. When she arrived at the big house where she was to work she was so over-awed by it all that she curtsied to the powdered footman who opened the door, thinking he was the gentleman of the house. She became the eighth of eight house-maids and slaved from 5 a.m. until late at night at all the roughest work. She had to scrub at the bare boarded floors of the staff rooms with a mixture of soft soap and silver sand until her hands, and arms up to her elbows were red raw. On most nights she cried herself to sleep.

To understand how children could be pressed into such ser-vitude, one has to recall the general economic conditions of the time. In the 1890s thousands of Londoners were homeless, sleep-ing in the parks, on the Embankment or in the recesses of London Bridge. However badly a servant might be accommodated, it was no doubt better than the prevailing housing conditions for the poor in the London of the 1890s as described by a minister, Joseph Ritson, in the *Primitive Methodist Magazine*. Of seven hundred families in Marylebone, three-quarters were forced to live packed together like sardines in single rooms. In London as a whole there were 50,000 families, each occupying only a single room 'and in most of them the conditions of health and morality are utterly absent.' Earlier in Victoria's reign, Marylebone had been classed as one of the seven 'black parishes' of London because half the women sent from the workhouses into domestic situations later became prostitutes. However oppressed in service, a girl would think twice about offending her employer when she could be cast out into the streets to face conditions such as these.

Lily Graham went into service in 1906, sixteen years later than Ellen Brown. She was aged thirteen, and started as a scullery maid at a house in Park Street, Mayfair. Her wages were £6 a year. In a letter to the author she vividly remembers that vanished age, arriving at the grand house in Mayfair just as the Pickford's carrier pulled up outside, watching her tin box (the only luggage that a servant girl was expected to have) being dragged down the area steps into the servants' hall. Deliveries of servants' trunks were not, of course, permitted at the front door. Later this trunk had to be taken up several flights of back stairs to the attic bedroom that Lily was to share with a housemaid and a tweeny.

Lily was born in 1893 and put into an orphanage at the age of seven, after her father died. Orphanages were the nurseries of servant girls, institutions where they could be trained for service with just enough part-time schooling to give them the basic 'three Rs': reading, writing and arithmetic. When Lily was put out into the world to earn her living at the age of eleven, she had to spend two years as a messenger and matcher at a dressmaker's to save enough money to buy the blue cotton dresses, white aprons and caps that were the necessary uniform when applying for a domestic situation.

Working conditions in Lily's time had improved only slightly. At the turn of the twentieth century scullery maids were staying in bed as late as 5.30 a.m. or even six before starting their day's work, instead of rising at four as their mothers and grandmothers had done! They also demanded, and received, a half day off *every week* and some were earning more than ten shillings (50p) a month. But apart from these changes, conditions were much as they had been for the previous fifty years. Servants still slept in the attics and worked in the basements and had little freedom and even less spare time.

There were changes in the world outside the servants' hall, of course. When Lily Graham went into service in 1906 a London transport operator, Thomas Tilling, had started building motor buses, double-deckers with solid tyres, acetylene lights and curtains at the windows, and the 'Twopenny Tube,' London's first underground electrified railway, was no longer a novelty. But London was still primarily a gaslit city, jammed with horse-drawn buses and carts, hansoms and clarences and private carriages. Most houses were lit by gas, or oil lamps and candles, because electric light was still regarded as a new-fangled nonsense, and it was expensive. Bathrooms and central heating were almost unheard of. The hip bath and coal fires in every room were the general rule, keeping those armies of maids busy staggering upstairs with scuttles of coal that produced smoke to thicken London's fog.

The tradesmen called at the door with daily supplies: the butcher drove a high dogcart; the baker brought bread in a large basket covered with a white cloth; and the milkman arrived in a pony-drawn chariot with two big churns on it, from which the milk was measured out into jugs. Muffin men plied their wares from door to door, carrying trays on their heads and ringing a handbell. The tinkling tunes of the barrel organ mingled with the street cries: 'Who'll buy my sweet lavender?' or 'Any old chairs to mend?' Gypsies would sit on the kerb while they re-caned the seats of chairs.

Few houses were equipped with gas stoves. Cooking was mostly done on vast coal-fired ranges that had to be black-leaded and the steel parts burnished with emery paper by the unfortunate 'tweeny' who rose before breakfast. The range also heated the hot water that would be carried upstairs in burnished copper and brass containers, as big as watering cans, for washing and bathing.

Victorian and Edwardian ladies expected, and received, service outside as well as inside their homes. On the railways they would travel first class, accompanied by servants travelling second class. Sometimes a sign reading 'For Second Class Passengers and Servants' was used by the railway companies to deter any mean-minded gentleman who might be tempted to buy a second class ticket and save money. The problems raised by segregation of the classes in trains were easily surmounted, as Frederick Gorst recounts in his book *Of Carriages and Kings*.

As a footman accompanying Her Ladyship to the family's country seat in Warwickshire in the early 1900s it was his duty to make a first class reservation for her and a second class one for himself. He carried several robes and steamer rugs to put over her knees and feet in the train because compartments were unheated. He also carried a hot water container to put under her feet. He was responsible for her jewel case, which he wore attached by a heavy steel chain to a silver bracelet locked on his wrist. Lady Howard was in the habit of travelling with pearls and diamonds worth as much as £100,000.

En route to Warwickshire from Paddington, Gorst served tea to Her Ladyship from a hamper. Whenever the train stopped at a station he went forward, running alongside the train, to ask: 'Is there something you wish, your Ladyship?' The reply was invariably: 'No, thank you Gorst. I am quite comfortable. Everything is quite all right.'

The Victorian and Edwardian passion for 'service' extended down the social scale to emporiums in the suburbs where shop walkers hovered at the entrances ready to dart forward and ask: 'What is your pleasure, Madam?' the moment a customer walked in. The lady would then be conducted to a chair at the counter of her choice, where the floorwalker would imperiously command an assistant: 'Forward please, Miss Jones.' When the purchase was complete the assistant would call out: 'Sign please,' and one of the floorwalkers would cast an eye over it and make an initial on the bill, which was then transported to the cashier's box in a container running on an overhead rail. The lady was then bowed out of the shop with a profusion of 'Thank you, Madams.'

There were jobs for girls in shops, as an alternative to domestic service. But they, too, were expected to work long hours for appallingly little pay. The first female typist had appeared in England in 1897 and there were growing opportunities for women in offices, but only for those who had the necessary basic education.

There was much talk of female emancipation and the 'new Woman,' in the first decade of the twentieth century. Her Grace the Duchess of Sutherland was 'actively interested in social questions and an ardent worker in causes for the amelioration of social conditions.' The first Labour Mayoress, Mrs Will Crooks, wife of the first working man Member of Parliament (for Woolwich), had made a tour of the Empire. And Lady Angela Forbes, a 'keen sportswoman and a brilliant member of Society,' had opened a florists' shop in George Street, Portman Square. (*Everywoman's Encyclopaedia*, Volume 2, 1910.) But there was still a considerable, some might have said unbridgeable, gap between the leisured ladies of quality who worked for causes or opened florists' shops as an amusing pastime and those who had to work to live.

The lives of the leisured classes usually revolved smoothly around certain events and annual rituals; shooting in Scotland, Cowes Week for yachting, the racing at Ascot. They either took their servants, or at least the upper servants, with them on their travels, or left them at the town house on 'board wages.' Spring cleaning, an arduous and exhausting annual event, was usually carried out while the 'family' was away.

The London Season, from the middle of May to the middle of August, was a time of lavish entertaining, with dinner parties, receptions and coming-out dances for daughters of marriageable age. A time for calling on friends and leaving cards, for scoring social points off rivals and snubbing those who were 'out.' For those below stairs the start of The Season signalled the arrival of an even heavier work-load, even later nights and earlier rising, than usual.

The author's mother, whose maiden name was Jenny Cole, was in service at Denmark Hill. There were seven daughters in the house so dances were frequent (an eligible young bachelor might find himself invited to as many as ten 'hops' in one evening). All fourteen servants were kept busy into the small hours, down in the basement, icing cakes, preparing elaborate sweets and confections, and tackling mountains of washing up. They were expected to be on call until the last guest had gone and the last daughter had gone upstairs to bed. However late they went to bed, the servants had to be up at the usual time in the morning.

At the turn of the twentieth century the rich were still very rich, and not the least shy about it. But although few of the rich had the merest apprehension of the social changes to come later in the century, there were continual complaints by employers that their servants were becoming too proud to do housework. *The Sphere* took up the refrain: 'The present condition of friction between mistress and maid is one totally destructive to domestic peace.

Home is rapidly becoming the place that one seeks only when it is impossible to go elsewhere. The servant who takes an interest in her work seems no longer to exist, and in return for high wages we get but superficial service. Where is the maid to be found who takes pride in the brilliance of the glass used upon the table or remembers of her own initiative to darn the damask? Every sort of contrivance now lessens labour – carpet sweepers, knife machines, bathrooms, lifts – in spite of these the life of a housewife is one long wrestle and failure to establish order.'

In fact, by 1911 there had been a noticeable drop in the number of domestic servants compared with the figures for 1891 (according to the Official Census for England and Wales). There were 1,271,990 women and girls employed as indoor servants: 114,277 fewer. Yet at the same time the population had grown by six million and with it the middle classes, made increasingly prosperous as trade with the far-flung Empire flourished and industry at home continued to expand. The new rich naturally wanted their complement of servants, yet the supply was shrinking. This shortage was perhaps the basis of servant-master friction.

One reason for the shortage of supply was the growing job opportunities for working class girls in shops and factories. Domestic service was still the main occupation of the female working population, but in the first decade of the twentieth century there were the first signs that the Great Age of Servants had passed its peak.

Another reason was the growth of mass education. In 1902 the Balfour Education Act had brought in secondary education, raising the school-leaving age from ten to twelve. In 1891 the Census had shown that more than 100,000 girls aged between ten and fifteen were in service. In the 1911 Census the figure was down to 39,413.

The Balfour reforms were long overdue and no more than was just and necessary. Before free compulsory education for all was introduced in the late 1890s, the poor had been taught as a charity, mainly by the Church of England and such organizations as the Ragged School Union and the National Temperance League. Parents had to pay as much as they could afford and as a result the majority of working class children received no education at all.

As E. S. Turner writes in *What the Butler Saw*: 'One deplorable result of popular education was that servant girls were publishing pamphlets criticizing their mistresses, claiming twelve free hours a week and all Sundays off, and even demanding that mistresses should produce references.'

Education also fostered the birth of the halfpenny newspaper, eager to cater for a newly literate mass audience. Young girls were thus made more aware of opportunities in other fields where they would at least have some time to call their own.

Many daughters of former servants nursed a sense of resentment towards their employers, not necessarily because they themselves were badly treated, but because of the tales they had heard from their mothers, relations and friends. Antagonism against 'them upstairs' was part of their social inheritance.

But there was also a more immediate basis to this antagonism as far as the early twentieth century servant was concerned. Although various Factory Acts, passed in Queen Victoria's reign, had made a start in tackling the dreadful problems of poverty and exploitation associated with the Industrial Revolution, there was no legislation to deal with oppression in domestic service. As E. S. Turner points out, while deploring the fact that shop girls were employed for fourteen hours a day, many mistresses kept their own servants on duty for sixteen and thought nothing of it.

Women of the Victorian and Edwardian middle classes regarded a life of complete idleness as being essential to maintaining their position in life. If they put a piece of coal on the fire, lifted a duster or answered a doorbell, they were 'letting their husbands down.' Or worse, depriving a needy person of employment. So, during the Great Age of Servants, a whole class of women was reared that was incapable of performing even the simplest domestic services for itself. These gentle mistresses never had to make a pot of tea, wash a cup, darn a sock, post a letter, or even brush their own hair.

In their homes and clubs, surrounded by antlers, leopards' heads, tiger skin rugs, elephants' feet made into umbrella stands and other trophies of the Empire-builders, the middle classes of the early 1900s discussed the servant problem. It was the perennial topic of conversation over the polite tinkle of teacups. But nevertheless, the servant problem had *always* provided a perennial topic of conversation for employers for as long as servants had been employed. It had always been difficult to get good servants and consolation was taken from the belief that the lower orders were notoriously ungrateful for the benefits of good 'situations' in service.

If employers felt an occasional shiver of apprehension of

changes in society that could not be entirely favourable to them, they did not show it to the world. Also, despite the difficulties of maintaining cheerful and efficient domestic staffs in the early years of the twentieth century, few middle class homes were without resident domestic help. Apart from being an important symbol of status, servants were a necessity in houses that had few labour-saving devices.

As for the servants, the majority in Edwardian England worked in conditions that were incomparably better than those of most working class families, at a time when there was no dole and no outdoor relief. A place in service was, by any standard, better than a place in the workhouse. Even though they lived-in with the employing family, sharing cramped quarters, working excessive hours for a few shillings reward, they were among the most favoured groups of the working class.

The rot finally set in to domestic service as a result of the First World War. Many women were drafted into factories to make munitions, or they drove trams, worked on the land and generally took over those jobs formerly reserved to men. But in the years leading up to the war, the servant problem had not assumed the proportions of a national 'crisis.' The 'lower classes' seemed as firmly convinced as ever that some were born to rule while the rest, the majority, served. Most servants were in no way bitter or resentful about this apparent fact of life.

This book examines in detail the world of 'upstairs' and 'downstairs' which has passed completely away.

2

NOT IN FRONT
OF THE SERVANTS

'Oh, Lord, keep us in our places.' Servants'
morning prayer.

The social attitude of employers towards domestic servants
described in a letter to the author from William H. Tait and Mrs
Helen Noel-Hill can be gathered from a mother's explanation to
her son that, while in their own way they were admirable people,
domestics were 'not quite our sort.' The daughter of a British Army
Colonel who returned from India to retirement on a small pension
in England, in 1905, remembers that her mother was always kind
to the one general servant, who was required to do all the housework and cooking in an eight-roomed house, but at the same time
looked upon her as an entirely different kind of being – not really
quite human, although a cut above the 'native.' In India this lady
had refused to employ an ayah (a native nurse) and had one of the
sergeants' wives for a nanny.

The behaviour of the middle classes at home was conditioned to
some extent by the constant presence of this inferior class. It was
sometimes inconvenient, but necessary, that they should be on
hand at all times because any work that had to be done, they had
to do. The 'family' – that is to say the master and mistress and their
children – were not to lift a finger for themselves. If the fire needed
making up, they rang the bell and the maid came running. If the
doorbell rang, no member of the family would dream of answering it – that is what maids were for. It all seemed perfectly natural,
not only to the employers but to the majority who made up the
servant class.

On most social occasions hostesses deemed it necessary to have
a respectable number of parlourmaids to wait at table. If really
confidential matters had to be discussed around the dinner table, a

contrivance called a 'dumb waiter' – a trolley with shelves that could be stocked with food and cutlery and left in the dining room for guests to help themselves – was available.

It was considered bad form to discuss the shortcomings of servants in their presence. The essential point was that although servants were clearly an inferior class it was not done to say so. That was vulgar, and vulgarity was something to abhor. The point is made by 'Vulgar Little Lady' in the 1868 edition of *Original Poems*:

'But, mamma, now,' said Charlotte, 'pray, don't you believe
That I'm better than Jenny, my nurse?
Only see my red shoes, and the lace on my sleeves;
Her clothes are a thousand times worse.

'I ride in my coach and have nothing to do,
And the country folks stare at me so;
And nobody dares to control me but you,
Because I'm a lady, you know.

'The servants are vulgar, and I am genteel;
So, really, 'tis out of the way,
To think that I should not be better a deal
Than maids, and such people as they.'

'Gentility, Charlotte,' her mother replied
'Belongs to no station or place;
And nothing's so vulgar as folly and pride,
Though dress'd in red slippers and lace.

'Not all the fine things that fine ladies possess
Should teach them the poor to despise;
For 'tis in good manners, and not in good dress,
That the truest gentility lies.'

But not all employers were capable of maintaining such a high standard of gentility, as Mrs Arthur found when she visited a certain Mrs Jones. Mrs Jones was constantly ringing for her servants and railing at them: 'Such a set! That girl has a habit of making me ring twice. It really seems to give them pleasure, I believe, to annoy one. Ah, me! This trouble with servants is never ending. It meets you at every turn.'

Mrs Arthur commented in *Home Scenes and Influences* (1866) that the girl was not spoken to during the whole meal except in a tone of anger or offensive authority, and she added: 'I was no longer surprised that Mrs Jones found it difficult to keep good domestics, for no one of feeling can long remain with a woman who speaks to them always in a tone of command, or who reproves them in the presence of visitors.'

Was it bad form to speak roughly to servants, or simply expedience to speak gently in case they gave notice and left?

It was mostly the new rich, who displayed vulgarity in their behaviour towards servants, possibly because they could rarely command the respect accorded to breeding and blue blood. The estates of dukes and earls in England were little principalities within whose borders His Grace or His Lordship wielded feudal powers. But the power was exercised in silken gloves, and aristocrats were usually quite at ease with their servants, having no need to constantly demonstrate their social superiority.

The upper classes relied on the total discretion of those who served them, a trust that was rarely misplaced. In 1911 a minor scandal arose following disclosures in *The Times* that a butler had been asked by an American woman journalist to supply items of gossip about the rich, the high-born and the famous who visited his employers' house. Needless to say, the butler did not avail himself of the offer, but told his mistress. The woman who tried to bribe him was, after all, *an American* . . .

In the Edwardian period it was felt that concern for the social welfare of the lower orders was admirable in a lady. A few made attempts at mixing socially with the lower classes. The Duchess of Portland, for example, held a fortnightly sewing class at Welbeck Abbey for miners' wives and served tea for them from a silver urn, while two footmen passed the sandwiches and cakes. Frederick Gorst, who was a footman at the time, recalls that some of the miners' wives treated the servants with the utmost disdain, as though they were duchesses themselves: others were uncomfortable in such august surroundings, and humble to the point of embarrassment. After the sewing class, the women queued to use the lavatory, revelling in the hot running water, the scented soap and embroidered towels. Her Grace very much enjoyed these occasions, says Gorst. 'We servants,' he goes on 'took a different view of the sewing class. All of us derived a good deal of amusement from these gatherings.' But they made sure the duchess didn't see them laughing.

In London Queen Alexandra instituted what she called Queen's Teas, to which ten thousand maids-of-all-work were invited, to be waited upon by ladies. The Countess of Aberdeen held drawing room tea parties for those who normally never emerged from below stairs. Sir James Barrie poked gentle fun at the idea in his comedy *The Admirable Crichton*, in which Lord Loam holds similar tea parties and orders his family to fraternize once a month with the servants' hall over tea in the drawing room. The daughters are reminded there must be no condescension – 'The first who condescends *recites*' – but as one of them complains: 'Even to think of entertaining the servants is so exhausting.'

Crichton, the butler, who is a Conservative, privately disapproves of Lord Loam's Radical views and finds him 'not sufficiently contemptuous of his inferiors.' At the monthly tea party, the master insists on equality and everybody hates it, not least the servants. The width of the chasm separating 'upstairs' from the servants' hall is revealed by Lord Brocklehurst's inquiry of the between-maid, in a desperate effort at conversation: 'And now tell me, have you been to the Opera? What sort of weather have you been having in the kitchen?'

When they are cast away on a desert island it is Crichton who takes command. He is a stronger character and more of a natural leader than his aristocratic employer. But once they are returned to the civilization of Edwardian London the recognized class barriers are restored. Crichton knows his place.

Most people regarded egalitarianism as a dangerous folly. A pamphlet published in 1859, entitled *Domestic Servants As They Are And As They Ought To Be*, explained that once servants began to measure their desires and their deserts by the doings of the class above them, they would place themselves on an assumed equality and there would be no possibility of meeting their demands. *The Spectator* suggested that '. . . one woman cannot do happily the will of another woman simply because it is her will, without looking up to her in some degree. . . . If domestic service is to be tolerable there must be an attitude of habitual deference on the one side and one of sympathetic protection on the other.'

But there were those, however few, who questioned the social attitudes that governed domestic service. Charles Booth, whose study of *Life and Labour in London* was published in 1889, said that domestic service revolted those accustomed to free speech. He wrote: 'From both servant and subject there is demanded an all-pervading attitude of watchful respect accompanied by a readiness to respond at once to any gracious advance that may be made, without ever presuming or for a moment "forgetting ourselves". . . .'

Servants were expected to be as nearly invisible and inaudible as was humanly possible when they appeared in 'the front of the house.' The rules were strict. These examples of just a few of them give a very clear idea of the social *apartheid* that existed in English homes of the period. They were taken from *Rules for the Manners of Servants in Good Families* (Ladies' Sanitary Association, 1901):

'*Do not* walk in the garden unless permitted, or unless you know that all the family are out; and be careful to walk quietly when there, and on no account to be noisy.

'Noisiness is considered bad manners.

'Always move quietly about the house, and do not let your voice be heard by the family unless necessary. Never sing or whistle at your work where the family would be likely to hear you.

'*Do not* call out from one room to another; and if you are a housemaid, be careful not only to do your work quietly, but to keep out of sight as much as possible.

'Never begin to talk to the ladies or gentlemen, unless it be to deliver a message or ask a necessary question, and then do it in as few words as possible.

'*Do not* talk to your fellow servants, or to the children of the family in the passages or sitting rooms, or in the presence of ladies and gentlemen, unless necessary, and then speak to them very quietly.

'When meeting any ladies or gentlemen about the house, stand back or move aside for them to pass.

'Always answer when you· receive an order or a reproof, either "Yes, Ma'am" or "I am very sorry, Ma'am," to show that you have listened.

'*Do not* speak to a lady or gentleman without saying "Ma'am," "Miss" or "Sir," as the case may be, and do not speak to ladies or gentlemen or their friends or of their private residences as "Green's" or "Turner's," say always "Mr" or "Mrs" or whatever the title may be, before the name.

'Always speak of the children of the family as "Master", "Miss."

'When you have to carry letters or small parcels to the family or visitors do so upon a small salver or hand tray. If obliged to take anything in the hand, or to lift it off the salver, do not give it to the person to whom it belongs, but lay it down on the table nearest to him or her.

'Should you be required to walk with a lady or gentleman, in order to carry a parcel, or otherwise, always keep a few paces behind.

'*Do not* smile at droll stories told in your presence, or seem in any way to notice, or enter into, the family conversation, or the talk at table, or with visitors; and do not offer any information unless asked, and then you must give it in as few words as possible. But if it is quite necessary to give some information unasked at table or before visitors, give it quietly to your master or mistress.'

The booklet advises servants to wash themselves *all over* once a day, to avoid *bad smells* (their italics) and to wear strong, decent underclothing. It initiates poor, ignorant little Mary Jane into the mysteries of 'At Home' and 'Not At Home' and warns her that 'there are many evil-minded persons who entice girls to their ruin by advertisements.'

It was all very well-meaning, but the employing class took little or no trouble to establish any personal relationship with their servants. Margaret Parry left home in 1927 at the age of fourteen and a half to enter domestic service as fourth housemaid in a large country house near Bath. Looking back, in a letter to the author, she finds it odd that employers took so little interest in their servants as *people*.

'We lived in their houses for years at a time and they knew nothing about us, except that we worked hard and were honest, which information they received from a previous employer. I cannot remember anyone ever asking about my home or family.'

Even the kindliest of employers seemed to regard their servants as chattels, thinking nothing, for instance, of changing their names arbitrarily if they happened to clash with those of 'the family.' Mary or Jane were common generic names for servant girls. Anything varying from the norm (Ada, or Marion, perhaps) was pretentious, and not allowed. The more senior female staff were addressed by their surnames only. In a letter to the author Mrs Stewart, of Evesham, remembers that in her grandmother's house, before 1900, maids were called by the names which that venerable lady had chosen for each position. Thus the head maid was *always* Emily, the next Jane, the cook Charlotte and the kitchenmaid Mary. Whatever their own names happened to be, they were ignored.

It was considered vitally important that domestics should not 'get above themselves.' *The Servants' Magazine*, for instance, printed in 1867 the following slogan, which it considered suitable for hanging in the kitchen: 'Never change your place unless the Lord clearly shows you it will be for your soul's good.'

But some servants were apt to give notice without consulting the Almighty first. The overall impression is of cowed inferiors shivering in apprehension at dismissal, but by no means all servants were frightened to answer back when they considered themselves wronged or ill-used by their masters, and the animosity between the domestic staff and 'them upstairs' was not always suppressed. Cooks were particularly touchy creatures, prone to fits of temperament and marching out in high dudgeon. As the humorist Saki wrily observed in 1904: 'She was a good cook as cooks go; and as cooks go, she went. . . .'

Employers undertook to provide free food and lodging for their servants, and in some cases clothing as well, in addition to paying a wage. To some extent, a life in service was sheltered from the cruel world outside. A servant could be sacked for laziness, or dishonesty, but as long as she 'knew her place' and did her work as it should be done, she was sure of her food and a roof over her head. Few other members of the English working class in Victorian and Edwardian times could boast of such security. Servants were not in any real sense part of the family whose roof they shared, but they *were* made to feel protected.

In return for a home many of them gave a lifetime of loyalty and devotion to those whom they genuinely regarded as their betters. Elsie Raum, a former maid who became a nanny, wrote to the author: 'I always respected my employers. In fact if I despised them as the writer Margaret Powell (author of *Below Stairs*) seems to have done, it would have been degrading to work for them. At the risk of being called old-fashioned – we all had our place and we knew it, and as a result the world seemed a happier place.'

Good servants had an innate dignity that made them respectful to other people, yet never servile. But because of their position many female servants were forced to remain spinsters all their lives because they had little or no free time or opportunity to meet young men. Their devotion to their masters lasted to the grave. One of the many letters the author received on this point told of a girl who served one mistress for more than thirty years, starting in the 1870s. Mrs W. Davison of Northwood writes: 'In my aunt's last illness when she suffered a stroke but lived semi-paralysed for many years, this devoted maid never left her mistress day and night. She brought her simple iron bedstead down from her attic bedroom and placed it at the foot of my aunt's bed. At my aunt's death it was the lowly maid who performed the last offices and rites. She would not allow anyone else to touch her. Her pay after many years was £30 a year.'

Cynics may argue that such loyalty was merely the result of economic pressures, or was created by the promises of a legacy or an annuity, promises that were not always kept. Nevertheless, many domestic servants did show a touching loyalty to the family they served. It is all the more surprising in view of the pittance they received for so much work and the small amount of leisure they were given.

Some, of course, were treated with almost incredible meanness. In a letter to the author a former maid recalls working for a family before, during and after the First World War, who scrimped and saved to such an extent that they even sold newspapers to the fishmonger to gain a few pence. The so-called ladies of the house gave the maid their cast-off clothes, but kept back money to pay for them out of her scanty wages. The house was wired for electricity, except for the maid's bedroom, where a candle had to do. She helped to nurse the master during a terminal illness and when he died he left her £50. Later she learned he had left a total of £32,000. Soon after that the mistress decided to sell up and live with her daughter, so the housemaid found herself without a job after nine years of service with the one family.

Recalling that time in old age she writes: 'Maids had no liberty, status or privileges. As I see it, the system was a continuation of slavery, except that you were able to hand in your notice and leave instead of having to stay for life. One did not dare answer back when lashed with the tongue or suffering humiliation. I always had to be allowed to post a letter at the letter box less than four hundred yards away. If one became ill, permission had to be obtained to attend a doctor's surgery. To my way of thinking, those were cruel unjust times. Let folk who imagine they were "good old days" look back with nostalgia to them. For me, the present.' (She asks in her letter: 'I would rather you did not use my name. To this day I blush at the thought of ever being sent to service.')

The great majority of the million and more servant girls worked not in stately homes or palaces but in relatively modest middle class homes. There the social barriers were most strictly maintained. A vicar's daughter remembers when she was about seventeen having two friends to tea and Mary the maid joining them as they sat on the lawn. Her mother was furious and promptly ordered Mary back to her place, in the kitchen.

The outwardly solid comfort of the Victorian and Edwardian middle class was overshadowed by a sense of insecurity. Despite their rising importance, the middle classes were neither respected nor feared. They voted Conservative but they were despised by the well-bred and fashionable, and the upper classes in London were worlds removed from the prosperous *bourgeoisie* of the suburbs and the provinces. The clean-living, thrifty and God-fearing inhabitants of Herne Hill, Clapham and Tooting were also despised by the great unwashed masses who lived in insanitary hovels nearer the city centre. C. F. E. Masterman in *The Condition of England* portrayed the fears of the middle class householder: 'The vision of a "Keir Hardie" in caricature – with red tie and defiant beard and cloth cap, and fierce, unquenchable thirst for middle class property – has become an image of Labour Triumphant which haunts his waking hours. He has difficulty with the plumber in the jerry-built house needing continuous patching and mending. His wife is harassed by the indifference or insolence of the domestic servant. From a blend of these two he has constructed in imagination the image of Democracy – a loud-voiced, independent, arrogant figure with a thirst for drink, and imperfect standards of decency, and a determination to be supported at someone else's expense. . . . He would never be surprised to find the crowd behind the red flag, surging up his little pleasant pathway, tearing down the railings, trampling the little garden; the "letting in of the jungle" upon the patch of fertile ground which has been redeemed from the wilderness.'

For all their fears of the lower classes, many middle class employers in gentle suburbia were particular to see that the girls of such origins who lived under their own roofs were treated civilly. They tried to model their manners on those of the aristocracy. A child could expect a good caning if he dared to call a maid a 'skivvy.'

In prosperous Victorian homes the younger children, of whom there were so very many, were subject to the same rules as the servants of the house. They – like the servants – were expected to be inaudible and invisible most of the time. Queen Victoria, as in many other matters, set the example of a calm, unruffled routine for large families, in which devotion to duty was all important.

> When little Fred went to bed,
> He always said his prayers.
> He kissed Mama and then Papa,
> And straightaway went upstairs.

Servants' territory behind the green baize doors seemed to hold a special fascination for the children of the family, possibly because they were forbidden to go there without permission.

Children, being children, were capable of seeing the servants as they were, diverse and often interesting personalities, not as merely utilitarian objects. Mrs Edith Melville-Steele, in a letter to the author, about her family's servants between the 1890s and 1920s, writes: 'Despite the great social differences we were genuinely fond of them, in a special sort of way, of course. I remember my brother and I pleading with mother to allow us to have tea in the kitchen with the maids. This privilege was granted us only about once a month.'

Mrs Mary Kilpatrick in a letter to the author about her childhood from 1900 on writes: 'Looking back one wonders at the pittance these domestics received for so much work . . . and yet, I remember these girls for the most part happy. We considered them friends.'

The gulf between nursery and drawing room widened with increasing middle class prosperity because more servants would be employed to take care of the children. So, it was often left to cook, nanny or the governess to think of the proper euphemisms to explain a death in the family to the children, or to deal tactfully with the 'facts of life' if and when awkward questions were asked. Sometimes at bathtime or bedtime the knowledge was imparted by an ignorant young servant girl without much knowledge herself. The earliest sexual fantasies of the author of *My Secret Life* (a book quoted from in more detail in Chapter 3) concerned the nurserymaid who bathed him and took him to the lavatory.

Like the servants who were not actually serving, children were not admitted to formal dinners and balls, or taken on visits to the Opera. Together, servants and children peered wide-eyed through the banisters at the guests in their finery arriving or departing into the night.

A humble scullery maid might never be seen at all by the mistress of the house, except at Christmas when she was taken upstairs and presented in solemn ritual to give a humble thanks for her present, a print dress length for her uniform to be made up at her own expense. Similarly, the children of the family might be presented once a month when there was an 'At Home' and friends called or left cards.

Miss Inez Pryor, another of the author's correspondents, remembers such rituals at her home in The Boltons, South Kensington, before the 1914–18 war: 'We children were dressed up for the occasion with white picqué coats and white boots and had to put in an appearance for a short time, which I might add, we all loathed. The silver teapot and the best china was all in evidence. . . . Looking back, I realize the appalling conditions of the attics (the servants' quarters), the lumpy flock mattresses, no light or heating and bitterly cold and cheerless – they went up at night with their candles after slaving all day. It was 1914 when the change came and they all left to go to make munitions and we thought ourselves lucky to get anyone to help us in that large house.

'One used to talk in a very "hush-hush" voice about "Poor Mrs So-and-so who only has a tweenie to help her." Many people today laugh at our generation for being so helpless, but they do not understand that we were not *allowed* to do things in case we upset the servants and were considered interfering. I remember being sent to bed because I was found in the kitchen. It was against the rules.'

The question springs to mind: did the servants have no children of their own? Not, it seems, while they were in service, a career that usually ended when a girl got married. As it became more difficult to find good servants, some were allowed to stay on but children of these marriages led a rather sad, halfway existence as some of the letters I have received testify.

Employers sometimes became very fond of servants' children, especially if they had none of their own. Occasionally they became the guardians of the children of servants who died. But generally the 'housekeeper's child' brought up in other people's houses had a lonely, unhappy life, constantly afraid to make any noise or do any damage to house or garden. The practice of keeping married couples in service never really became established.

In a usually vain attempt to keep young girls in service as long as possible, employers tried to impose the life of the nunnery upon them. 'No followers' was the harsh edict that appeared again and again in the Domestic Situations Vacant columns. But, it failed to prevent most young servant girls finding husbands and leaving service to raise families of their own.

3

A FATE WORSE THAN DEATH

If you are in a great family, and my
lady's woman, my lord may probably like you,
although you are not half so handsome as
his own lady.

Jonathan Swift wrote the above-quoted words in his *Directions to Servants* in 1745, when sexual attitudes were a great deal more explicit than in the period covered by this book. He goes on to advise the lady's maid to get as much out of her master as she possibly can – 'never allow him the smallest liberty, not the squeezing of your hand, unless he puts a guinea into it' – and he advises an ascending scale of payments up to a hundred guineas, or a settlement of £20 a year for life, for granting what eighteenth-century bucks called the 'last favour.'

Such candid advice to waiting maids certainly held good in the Victorian era. But it would not have been *said* because by then relations between men and women of the same class, let alone those carried on clandestinely below stairs, had become shrouded in a fog of protocol as dense as any London pea-souper of the day. If a girl so much as went in a hansom cab alone with a man who was not her father, or old enough to be her grandfather, she was a fallen woman. The conventions militated against a young unmarried man and woman ever being alone together unless they were engaged, and all respectable girls were warned against males who would try to lure them to what was described as a 'fate worse than death.'

Sir Charles Petrie observes in *The Victorians*: 'The effect of these taboos was to drive the young man of the classes in question to somewhat sordid intrigues in other quarters. Readers of *Mary*

Barton and *The Newcomes* will remember how young Carson and Barnes Newcome treated the girls of a lower social status than their own. Youths in their teens were apt to take rank among their fellows according to their alleged triumphs over what were generally termed 'skivvies' or shop-girls, and such conditions were not good for either party, while in the presence of women of their own rank in life they were too often diffident and tongue-tied. It would be rash to dogmatize in these matters, but it is difficult to resist the conclusion that the Victorian segregation of the sexes in what was then termed "polite society" occasioned just as many *liaisons* of one sort and another as have marked more recent generations, even if not so much was said about them.'

Divorce or a broken engagement was socially disastrous and the Victorians expected their unmarried young ladies to remain in a state of simpering virginity. Even when they were married they were kept in a sort of nursery cocoon and expected to faint when faced with life's rougher edges. The well brought up Victorian girl walked up the aisle in total ignorance of the practical side of being a wife and with scarcely an idea of the value of money, how to organize a household budget or control her servants. In her own interest, as well as for reasons of morality, she was concerned to protect the virginity of the females below stairs by insisting upon 'no followers.' These girls were often pretty little things, so every effort was made to hide their feminine charms behind the plainest and most stiffly starched uniform that could be found.

As a policy of protection it was doomed to failure. The mistress of the house could keep undesirable callers away but not the predatory males of her own family. So while making the most strenuous effort to prevent the maids from consorting with boys of their own class, she was often forced to turn a blind eye to the philanderings of her own husband or sons. If, as happened all too often, a servant girl became pregnant by one of the family, the blame was placed squarely on her shoulders, not his.

My Secret Life, the eleven-volume memoirs of an anonymous Victorian gentleman, printed in Amsterdam around 1890, throws some light on the attitudes of his class towards female servants. In early adolescence he was surrounded by them and according to his account they all accepted his amorous advances: 'I had a soft voice and have heard, an insinuating way, was timorous, feared repulse, and above all being found out; yet I succeeded. Some of the servants must have liked it, who called me a foolish boy at first;

43

for they would stop with me on a landing, or in a room, when we were alone, and let me kiss them for a minute altogether.'

He was ordered by his mother to stop speaking to the servants, except when he wanted something. He obeyed the command to the letter and was then rebuked for being too imperious. His mother told him to speak to the servants 'respectfully'. He doubted whether his mother suspected that he was kissing and fondling them whenever he got the chance; in any event she took no steps to keep him away from the servants.

It is possible that having warned him his mother simply did not want to know what he was doing. The servants would not dare report him because that would mean losing their situation and their character. So the young master proceeded with his wenching, lurking around the back stairs and peeping through the keyholes of the maid-servants' quarters.

Later his father lost his fortune and died, and with the family's decline in status there were fewer servants about the house. But this merely served to give him greater opportunities for getting on intimate terms with them, graduating from fumbling advances towards an older girl to seduction of a maid of about his own tender age. He goes on to further conquests, most of them servants and other working class girls. He describes each amorous adventure in detail, and with evident relish.

One of the first maids he dallied with gave him 'lots of opportunities which my timidity prevented me from availing myself of. One day she said: "You're not game for much, although you are so big," and then kissed me long and furiously, but I never saw her wants, nor my chances that I now know of, though I see now plainly enough that, boy as I was, she wanted me to mount her.' He is at that stage rather frightened of sex but he gets bolder. One evening when he finds the girl alone in the kitchen doing some needlework by candlelight: 'I talked, kissed, coaxed her, began to pull up her clothes, and it ended in her running round the kitchen and my chasing her; both laughing and stopping at intervals, to hear if my aunt knocked.' The petting and fumbling proceeds, but the author is not mature enough to complete his conquest and feels ashamed of his inadequacy. Despite his shame, he continues to sneak into the kitchen whenever he can get the girl alone and during one such encounter he suggests: 'Let's do it!' but she mocks him: 'Lor! You ain't man enough.' It is clear that the maid is a willing tutor and when he graduates to seduction in his own right, he claims to have had no difficulty in finding compliant victims: 'As to servants and women of the humbler class . . . they all took cock on the quiet and were proud of having a gentleman to cover them. Such was the opinion of men in my class of life and of my age. My experience with my mothers' servants corroborated it,' and in another passage: 'I have now had many servants in my time, and know no better companions in amorous amusements. They have rarely lost all modesty, a new lover is a treat and a fresh experience to them. . . .'

It is worth remembering that while this was going on behind the scenes in an unknown number of outwardly respectable Victorian households, the employers were constantly being exhorted by ministers of the Church to make sure that their servants regularly attended divine worship. They were also urged to provide their young servant girls with a few well-chosen 'improving' books, such as: *The Servant's Friend*, *Girl's Own Annual*, *Handy Book for the Young General Servant* and so on. Most employers subscribed to the ideal of safeguarding the spiritual health of those in their care. The physical welfare of the young girls who slaved in the damp dungeons called kitchens was left to take care of itself.

The pursuit of servant girls, so graphically described in *My Secret Life*, seems to have been almost an upper class national sport, conducted under cover and according to no rules. In *The Other Victorians*, Stephen Marcus comments: 'One of the most striking things about such passages is how they reveal to us a number of assumptions that governed the relations of masters and servants. It is assumed by everyone, including the servants, that the author has a right to be doing what he is doing; if he is caught at it the consequences will fall entirely on her. . . . The language he uses to describe them is that of the horse-fancier or stableman; "a nice fresh servant" is "clean, well-fed, full-blooded," has not been used, ridden or raced for a week, and is ready for service. One need only be aggressive, importunate, masterful enough, and the animal is yours.'

All social barriers vanished when sex was the objective. On these occasions, as the author of *My Secret Life* points out, a washerwoman could banter with a prince, without the prince feeling in the least offended. Unfortunately his liberation from sexual 'hang-ups' is not accompanied by any radical ideas about class. In bed it means nothing to him. At all other times he applies the distinctions unthinkingly as in one passage where he describes a working girl who is 'commonly but comfortably clad, not warmly enough perhaps for well-to-do people, but enough so for her class who don't feel the cold as we do.'

We have no way of knowing how typical was his behaviour, although we have his own assertion that his opinions are shared by men in his class of life and of his age. Even after he was married he continued to find his pleasure among the female domestics in his household. After one encounter with Mary, a young servant employed by his wife, he described how she 'put quite down her clothes, and sitting up on the sofa gave me a kiss, said, "I must go and see about laying the things for dinner," and off she went. . . .'

On another occasion, when his wife has discovered a servant in some minor sexual irregularity and dismissed her, he comments: 'That, I quite expected, for it was the Mistress' custom to coax out the facts from the poor devils in a kind way, and then to kick them out mercilessly. Middle-aged married women are always hard upon the young in matters of copulation.'

Yet he showed scant mercy himself when he was called upon to play the part of the stern Victorian *pater familias*. James, a man-servant in his house, was caught 'in loving familiarities' with a servant girl called Lucy: 'The poor girl had let this out to the cook or someone else, and the cook split upon her. James was imprudent and denied it all, but I think the case was proved. It would not have done to have passed over open fornication. Had I done so, the habit would have spread through the household; so I reluctantly gave him notice. The poor girl went off very quietly in tears.

After his confessions of lechery on his own part, his concern about fornication 'spreading through the household' almost takes one's breath away as a piece of monumental hypocrisy. But he is about to rise to even greater heights. Lucy, the poor girl, was unable to get another situation and was in desperate straits. The master went to see her and seduced her, as one might have expected. He then procured an abortion, got James to marry the girl and packed them both off to a distant part of the country with £50 as a present.

It seems overdrawn, even as melodrama in the Victorian style, but the author assures us that these events actually took place. If he is telling the truth, the depravity shown in underground pornographic books of the period, or glimpsed in pier-end machines labelled 'What the Butler Saw', are a mirror of what went on behind the self-righteously moral façade, not mere fantasy.

In a conversation the author had with Mrs Ruth Sherren, whose father and grandfatner were Harley Street surgeons, she recalled an extraordinary incident concerning a parlourmaid in her grandmother's London household in the 1880s. It seems the girl served luncheon as usual, without appearing in any way disturbed or unwell, but failed to put in an appearance when the family sat down to dinner. Another maid was sent up to the attic to find her and came back with the startling news: 'Ooh, Mum, there's a baby in her room.' The girl, living in an eminent doctor's house, had delivered herself of a baby, without help of any kind, in the few hours between lunch and dinner. No one had noticed her condition, although in those days of very full skirts with hems touching the floor it was perhaps more difficult to detect a pregnancy.

Mrs Sherren does not know what became of the girl, although she feels sure that her grandfather, being a humane man, would not have turned her out into the streets. Instant dismissal was the fate of most girls who got into a similar plight. In the eighteenth century many an unmarried expectant mother was sent off to London in the first available wagon so that they would not become a burden on the local rates. Parish officers showed little mercy in such cases. If the girl was lucky she might find a situation as a scullery maid until her condition was discovered and then she would be turned out. A letter to the *London Chronicle* in 1758 said that when a servant's misconduct made it difficult for her to get another place she simply went out of town and returned with the next wagon. The letter goes on: 'And being made free of the wagon (which is the phrase among those sort of gentry for the "last favour") the honest fellow gives her a character.'

Without a reference, a maid stood no chance of getting another situation. If her family refused to take her in, she was faced with the alternative of the workhouse or prostitution. A large number of the 80,000 prostitutes in London in 1867 were former servants who had chosen the latter alternative. They were known as Dolly Mops and there was a great deal of liberal concern over these 'fallen women.' When Mr Gladstone was Prime Minister he walked the London streets at night trying to help them and offering to take them home to tea.

Another highly respectable Victorian gentleman who took an academic interest in the women of the lower classes was Arthur J. Munby, barrister, poet and civil servant. He interviewed and studied them and collected photographs and drawings. When he died in 1910 it became known that he had secretly married his servant, Hannah, a charity school girl, thirty-seven years previously. It caused a sensation and the story covered four columns in the *Daily Mirror*:

ROMANCE OF BARRISTER'S MARRIAGE
Further Light on Remarkable
Will Disclosure
WIFE AND SERVANT
Verses Upholding His Choice
Against World's Criticism
COTTAGES IN COUNTRY

What was *not* known at that time, because Munby's will contained the proviso that his diaries and documents must not be opened until 1950, was the extent of his 'eccentricity', as it would have appeared then. These diaries were published for the first time in 1972 and the entry for 23 November 1860 shows his unconventional attitude towards servant girls: 'Went to Clapham to dine with the Ellises. Georgie as usual intelligent and charming. . . . I look on Georgie with interest and affection, because *they say* she would marry me if I asked her. And truly she would make a wife to be proud of. Two pleasant Miss Johnstones were staying there: and all these young ladies, white bosomed, fairylike with muslin and flowers, found a foil for their elegance in a pretty but coarse-made rustic & red-handed waiting maid.

'Gentle, and beautiful in face as they – and her name *Laura* – why should she have a life so different? Why should she wear a cotton frock and a cap and hand me dishes – and why should those imperious misses order her about so? . . . This girl's large eyes have glanced at me furtively before: and tonight, as the young ladies crowd to the hall door and I am helping grandmamma to her carriage, Laura, waiting in the background, says low "Let me carry your bag, Sir" – and I give it her: and in the dusk outside she holds the carriage door open for me – and as she closes it and gives me the bag, somehow her thick broad hand comes more than once in contact with mine, and does not retreat. Oh ho! Here we have a scene for a novel: the hero from his chariot bows farewell to the elegant imperial creature who thinks she holds him captive, but meanwhile his real adieus are given, in secret pressure of her working hand, to the humble serving maid who hands him to the door! . . .'

His courting of 'Hannah Cullwick, servant,' as she was described in his will, was also a secret affair and he describes going to meet her at Kilburn, where she worked. She was already out in the street, wearing her old bonnet and working dress, but they could not even exchange a word of greeting in case somebody who knew her as Mr So-and-so's servant spotted them. They walked down side roads, among the unfinished houses, looking for somewhere to talk, with Hannah walking a few paces behind.

But they could find nowhere private enough, there were prying eyes everywhere, so in the end they turned back, with Hannah still walking slightly behind, off the path, and Mr Munby, barrister, talking to her hurriedly and nervously over his shoulder! Without one kiss or even a touch of the hand, Hannah went back to her kitchen and he made his way home. She called him 'Massa' and despite the oddities of their courtship they were much in love. Despite all their efforts to keep their liaison secret, it was discovered by a footman at the house in Norfolk Square, Bayswater, where Hannah was then working as a cook. She described in her own diary how she was dismissed:

'... one Sunday Massa came & walked to & fro past the house waiting for me to come out, & this man Gower had once lived at Massa's relations in Hyde Park Square & so knew him well, & again i gave my letters to the butcher boy to post when i couldn't get out, it seems this Gower ask'd him to let him look, & *that* settled his suspicions at once, & he & the house-maid both told Mr Sanders of it – what they said i don't know exactly but making out i was living dishonestly and so i was surprised & grievously hurt when i was rung for to see the Master, & he at once gave me notice to leave. I ask'd him *why* – he said, ''It's a painful thing to talk about, & i am very sorry, for Mrs S. likes you so much in the kitchen,'' and he didn't seem to like telling me, but i guessed what it was about & wished to right myself if i could ...

'So he said – ''You are keeping company with a gentleman – Gower has told me as *truth*.'' I said ''Yes Sir, it *is* true – i have for a great many years, & he's a gentleman in every sense of the word, even as you are. ...'''

Mr Munby courted his servant for *eighteen years* before he felt able to confide his love for her to his father, begging him at the same time not to tell the mother. His father was so overwhelmed with shame and horror at the news that his son was in love with a *servant*, that Munby never mentioned it again. When he married in

1873, he did so in secret. Although they lived together at his chambers in the Temple, Hannah insisted on remaining as a servant. When friends called, Munby was in the curious position of having to treat her as such, instead of presenting her as his wife.

As a matter of course, Hannah as the servant was ignored by any company that called on a social visit. But she, content to serve and having no wish to 'better herself,' continued to wait at table and say 'Sir' to her husband when she was spoken to. Only when they were alone did they behave as a normal, happily married couple, which, despite everything, they were, until the strain of the deception they had been forced into proved too much. Hannah went back to her native Shropshire on doctor's orders and for several years they were estranged until Munby bought a cottage for her, and visited her for three or four months each year.

Society would not allow them to break down the barriers that divided class from class. Hannah refused, like the heroine of *Pygmalion*, to become a *lady*, and Munby knew that if he made his marriage known to his family and the world at large he would be completely cast out. The couple died within six months of each other and, as Hannah herself predicted, theirs was a story that, a hundred years on, would seem incredible.

Most serving maids managed, despite all the deterrents and obstacles placed in their way, to meet and fall in love with somebody at more or less their own level in society. But the peculiarly Victorian attitudes to relations between the sexes, at whatever level, persisted well into the next generation. As late as the 1930s servant girls were still being made pregnant by close relatives of their employers, and then sacked for it. The employers still referred to any male friend of their female servants as a 'follower'.

Margaret Powell comments on this in her book *Below Stairs*: 'It was a funny thing that although none of them really liked you to leave if you were going to another job, if you left to get married it was a totally different thing. It was acceptable and it was respectable. And yet the business of getting a young man was not respectable, and one's employers tended to degrade any relationship. Their daughters were debs, and they could meet young men at balls, dances and private parties, but if any of the servants had boyfriends they were known as "followers". I think "followers" is a degrading term. . . .

'They could have said: "If you have a young man you're interested in, you can ask him in to the servants' hall when you've finished your work.'' But no, you had to slink up the area steps and meet him on the corner of the road on some pretext like going to post a letter. And on your night out when you came back you couldn't stand at the top of the area steps with him or bring him down to say goodnight to him. He wasn't a young man, he was a "follower". They made you feel there was something intrinsically bad in having a member of the opposite sex interested in you at all.'

The period she is recalling is not the high noon of Victoria's reign but the 1920s, the gay, anything goes twenties when skirts shot up and women were supposed to have been emancipated. Yet those who were in service at that time were labelled 'flighty' if they used the slightest trace of make-up, or coloured silk stockings when they were off duty, instead of 'nigger brown' ones.

In a letter to the author, Doris Hazell, who was a 'tweeny' in the 1930s, recalls: 'We were not allowed to wear artificial silk knickers as the slight swishing noise they made "disturbed" milady and might give "wrong ideas" to the menservants. . . . The Head Parlourmaid and Head Housemaid were allowed to wear black artificial silk stockings after lunch only (and they weren't permitted to produce that "disturbing" noise either!).'

A 'fate worse than death' awaited flighty servants. They became pregnant, like Agnes, an under parlourmaid, described by Margaret Powell in her book *Below Stairs*, who bought bottles of pennyroyal pills, Beecham's pills and quinine in desperate attempts to get rid of her unborn and unwanted child. She also tried mustard baths, jumping on and off park benches and shifting heavy furniture, all to no avail. When her condition was discovered she was told to leave at the end of the week. But Madam did give her a month's wages and this confirmed the other servants' suspicions that the father of the baby was the mistress's nephew, an extremely handsome young man. He had been spotted several times on the back stairs, which led nowhere but to the maids' bedrooms, and he had given Agnes *silk* underwear. This was a familiar situation in households employing servants as recently as forty years ago. Young working class girls were brought up with the idea that sex outside marriage was a deadly sin. Fear of the consequences kept most of them on the straight and narrow path. But a few succumbed, and paid dearly for it.

Fortunately for young girls in service almost every item of food was delivered to the door, and that meant that the boys and young men who delivered it were accessible to the denizens of the basement. Maids could spend a wholly enjoyable quarter of an hour chatting at the door to the butcher's boy, or create an exciting rivalry between him and the garden boy, or the boy who cleaned the boots, jousting like bold knights for the favour of her attentions.

One of the author's correspondents, Mr E. W. E. Booth, recalls a maid employed by his parents about 1900 who 'got into trouble' with a travelling greengrocer, a man with a horse and cart who came round selling at the door. The mistress saw him and told him to marry the girl, which he did.

Violet Turner, writing to the author from Faversham of her pre-First World War days in service, says: 'There was nowhere to go on my evenings out, only walking the country lanes and also to church on Sundays. We weren't allowed a young man near the house, but I always let the cook's young man in the back door on Friday evenings.'

A lady who was third housemaid in a country house in Lincolnshire in 1913 writes: 'The butler gave me more than one kiss as we passed in the back passage upstairs. I used to smile at him if he came in the Servants' Hall to complain of noise after supper. The head housemaid said: "How dare you smile at the butler." I think he was always afraid of me giving him away. I never did.'

A housemaid at a house in Hampshire remembers how she met her husband there. He was second gardener of twelve and he used to come indoors every day to see to the flowers and plants.

In 1911 Mrs Kate Brown (writing from Horsham) was dismissed from her job as a parlourmaid because she committed the grievous sin of having her boyfriend in to see her: 'Of course, it was forbidden in those days in case your sweetheart might be a burglar. They could never imagine a servant choosing someone respectable.' But as she goes on to point out in her letter, her future husband happened to be a baker in Fulham Road, London.

Margaret Lloyd-Philipps, writing from Tenby, recalls the strict rules in the house of her father, a parson in the 1890s: 'Followers were not allowed so it was difficult for them (the servants) to get married. Although I remember a cook of ours who was allowed to have her soldier fiancé from the nearby barracks to tea in the kitchen on Sundays, and she did marry her sergeant. I was then very small, about three, but I admired him with his red coat and his huge moustache.'

Mrs Rumble, of Coley Park, says that her father, who was in the Coldstream Guards at Wellington Barracks in the early 1900s, used to call at Lancaster Gate where her mother was in service and rattle his short cane on the iron railings: 'At this signal mother would shed cap and apron and excuse herself.'

The joys of courting seemed sweeter because the employers made it so difficult, and no amount of petty rules concerning 'followers' could prevent young servants finding themselves boy-friends. Mabel Johnson, who worked as an under nurse at a house in Nuneaton in 1912, wrote to the author from St Petersburg, Florida, where she now lives: 'It took me fifty years to figure out why I was released from that job. The much-married coachman was paying too much attention to me and I was lingering longer and longer each day in the coach-house where the pram was kept and which I had to keep clean and shining.

'Life in service was a good deal like life in a convent. I look back now and marvel at the extremity of our innocence and naiveté. Sex was something we didn't know about until marriage.'

Their lives were indeed sheltered from the nastiness of much of the Victorian and Edwardian working class life. For many a kitchenmaid or 'tweeny' her main contact with the larger world outside was at the tradesman's door where almost every item of food was delivered. And that world was bounded by the wrought iron railings at the top of the area steps.

4

THE DIVINE ORDER

Exhort servants to be obedient unto their
own masters, and to please them well in
all things . . .

(Titus *ii*. 9.)

Biblical texts were used in Victorian times as a form of propaganda, or indoctrination, to keep the lower orders in their place. In the case of domestic servants, the object was to show them that it was the will of the Almighty that they should stay in servitude and not complain; that domestic service was esteemed by the Lord as a service to Himself, which would be well rewarded in the next world, if not in this.

Indeed, before Queen Victoria came to the throne the Established Church had used its powerful influence to these ends, usually through the individual exhortations of its clergymen. They, of course, had a vested interest in keeping the domestic servant class properly subservient because they themselves needed at least a small staff to run the rectory or vicarage. Between 1776 and 1802 the Reverend James Woodforde found that on £300 a year it was possible to have the following staff: a farming man, who also helped about the house on occasion, a footman, a yard boy, an upper maid (who did the cooking) and an undermaid. The average country parson made do with a footboy who could tend to the livestock, milk the cows, churn butter, weed the garden, clean the shoes, run errands and wait at table, a maid-of-all-work and a cook.

Clergymen's wives ran frugal households, very much on the lines of 'waste not, want not,' and their husbands were of a practical turn of mind when dealing with domestics on matters other than spiritual. One early nineteenth century cleric, the Reverend John Trusler, urged employers to hire their servants by the year, rather than by the month, and not to pay them until the twelvemonth was up. This system, he observed, 'purchased respect.'

A London vicar, the Reverend Watkins, who was prominent in the Society for the Encouragement of Faithful Female Servants (which in a later age would have been almost, but not quite, SERFS for short), set up a free registry in 1813. Its object was to 'secure the young and unwary but virtuous female from the danger of resorting to *common* registry offices and to promote mutual tenderness, good-will and confidence among the superior and subordinate branches of a family.' The good vicar took a hard line against allowing servant girls to meet their friends on a Sunday because, he warned, 'Sabbath pleasures put a young woman in the highway of danger – and of ruin.'

In fact an astonishing number of pious tracts and cautionary tales were heaped on the heads of young serving maids. Titles such as *A Present for Servants*, and *Serious Advice and Warning to Servants*, speak for themselves, and one wonders what amount of their meagre spare time these hard-worked maids gave to studying them.

One such tract, *The Servant's Friend* by Mrs Trimmer, has been loaned to the author by K. M. Evans of Exmouth, Devon. It is in the form of an 'exemplary tale designed to enforce the religious instructions given at Sunday and other charity schools, by pointing out the practical application of them in a state of service.'

The hero is Thomas Simpkins, an 'exceedingly dutiful good child,' the comfort of his father and mother, who were very industrious, honest people who taught him to *fear and serve God* and *to do unto others as he would they should do unto him*. He never neglected to say his prayers morning and evening, nor on any account missed going to church twice a day on Sundays, unless prevented by illness, or attending on his father and mother, if they chanced to be sick.

When he is hired as a foot boy at the Rectory, the Reverend gentleman tells him what is expected of him: 'You will not find me, Thomas, like many masters, indifferent in respect of what becomes of your soul, so that you do the work I hired you for; on the contrary, I shall endeavour to give you such religious instructions as you stand in need of; shall allow you time to serve God; and will treat you kindly and justly in every respect.

'Now in return for this I have a right to expect you to serve me with fidelity. Every state and condition of life, Thomas, has its particular duties. The duty of a servant is to be obedient, diligent, sober, just, honest, frugal, orderly in his behaviour, submissive and respectful towards his master and mistress, and kind to his fellow servants; he must also be contented in his station, because it is necessary that some should be above others in this world; and it was the will of the Almighty to place you in a state of servitude.'

There is more in similar vein until the tale gets to its dramatic interest, a new cook called Susan, who instead of reading the Bible and other good books of an evening prefers histories 'full of nonsense about lords and ladies and squires falling in love with one another,' indecent ballads and books that tell fortunes. She also plays cards, rifles the drinks store and gets dressed up on a Sunday in a silk gown with a flounced petticoat and long train, with curls at her ears and her hair halfway down her back. Needless to say, she ends up on the streets in London, while Thomas marries a virtuous maid called Kitty and gets the tenancy of a farm owned by Squire Harvey.

As late as 1909 the author of the *Handy Book for the Young General Servant*, Mrs Barker (a book loaned to the author by Miss Muriel Maynard of Kew) was still unable to describe how to set a breakfast table, how to make a bed or how to wash up the dinner things without prefacing each duty with an improving text or verse. Instructions on how to dust are introduced with the following lines:

> Teach me, my God and King,
> In all things Thee to see,
> And what I do in anything,
> To do it as for Thee.
>
> A servant with this clause
> Makes drudgery divine;
> Who sweeps a room as for Thy laws,
> Makes that and the action fine.
>
> GEORGE HERBERT.

A decade before this book was published there had been a movement away from family prayers and church-going. King Edward VII had led the movement towards weekends out of town and the race-course when he was Prince of Wales, and he continued the trend as a fun-loving monarch. It was no doubt an understandable reaction against the style of his pious parents. The minister at Crathie Church noted that in all the thirteen seasons

Queen Victoria and her husband spent at Balmoral, Albert was only twice absent from the church which the royal couple attended with their numerous children and the entire retinue of servants. The parson pointedly referred to it as: 'A beautiful example in more ways than one to the great and noble of the land.'

Whatever the trend of the 'smart set' in the 1890s and the Edwardian era towards levity, the middle classes clung tenaciously to the solid Victorian virtues. Great stress was placed on the importance of servants regularly attending church with the family. But they were, of course, seated separately in the house of God, the servants in their own pews at the back, well away from those at the front reserved for their employers: 'We had to attend church every Sunday morning dressed in black and sit behind our employers' (anonymous writer of letter to the author, on being a housemaid in 1905).

Servants were relegated to the back of the church, or the gallery, because if they had been allowed to use the pews at the front, ladies and gentlemen would have stopped going and sought another place of worship. Even in heaven, it was assumed, the class barriers would be maintained.

The habits instilled into young girls in service have in many cases lasted a lifetime. Mrs Isabel Adams is eighty-two and still lives at Putney Heath where she was put into 'gentleman's service' at thirteen. The house where she remembers crying herself to sleep each night in her attic room has been pulled down to make way for a block of flats. But she treasures the Bible she was given as a Christmas present at the Bible class she was sent to on Sunday afternoons. Her husband, now dead, carried it with him in the trenches of Flanders in the 1914–18 war and she writes to the author: 'It's as good now as the day I was given it. I would like you to see it, all done up to keep it clean.'

Servants were not allowed to get themselves up in any finery for going to church, as ladies did. They had to dress in plain, sombre clothes, which amounted to an outdoor uniform denoting their station as domestics. Miss Doris Bodger, who started as a tweeny in a stately home at thirteen, told the author: 'For church on Sundays we had to wear black coats and skirts, black shoes, stockings and gloves, and a hat which was called a toque which made a young girl of thirteen look like a grandmother.'

Miss Chubb, writing from her home in Devon, recalls that when she worked as a tweeny in 1909 in a clergyman's house there were prayers every day, church on Sunday morning and she was expected to go in the evening on her Sunday off. A Bible class was also taken by one of the daughters of the house.

In the 1920s a country vicar invited his parishioners to send their domestics to church on a weekday afternoon, as well as on Sundays, on condition that he would promise to get them home in time to serve tea. And a seaside boarding house with aspirations to higher status had a notice in the hall asking the guests to bear with a cold meal on Sunday 'to allow the staff time to attend church.' The 'staff' consisted of one very much overworked maid! Mrs Nellie McIntyre, in a letter to the author from Coleraine, Northern Ireland, recalls working as a tweeny in a bishop's house where all the staff had to go to the dining room for prayers at 10 a.m., and again to the drawing room at 9.30 p.m.

Before 'days out' became general practice in service, the visits to church were sometimes the only outings a servant ever had. Many of them comment in their letters to the author that they liked going because it was their one escape from work.

The majority of employers in England insisted upon their living-in servants being members of the Church of England. No chapel-goers were employed by these pillars of the Established Church and certainly no Catholics. Governesses and ladies' maids applying for positions in the mid-Victorian period often stated in advertisements that they were members of the Established Church, and in *The Times* an advertisement for a master for a Ragged School in the London suburbs stated: 'The population is Roman Catholic, and the post a missionary one. Candidates must possess earnestness, tact, some experience in visiting among the demoralized poor, and above all, a sincere desire for the conversion of souls.'

Victorian newspaper advertisements for the better sort of domestic servants frequently added: 'No Irish need apply.' But this was probably only partly religious prejudice. Girls from the poorest parts of Ireland often had no idea of how to tackle anything but the most basic domestic tasks.

Yet if Catholics were beyond the pale to most middle class English households, Baptists and Methodists were little better. Even so the Nonconformist church had a strong influence among servants as the next few passages show.

On the Sunday after a valet, François Courvoisier, was hanged for the murder of his master, Lord William Russell, in 1840, the Reverend George Clayton delivered a thundering sermon at the York Street Chapel, Walworth, addressed especially to domestic servants. He took as his text Psalm xix. 13: 'Keep back thy servant also from presumptuous sins.'

The sermon began: 'These words have been selected with a view to the instruction and improvement of a numerous and interesting body of persons in society – those whom divine providence has placed in the condition of servants. Many of these are truly respectable, both for their character and for the conscientious and acceptable manner in which they discharge the duties they owe to their employers and to each other. But there are those, who are of an opposite description and a different class; who are a grief and disturbance to the families where they live, and who are often the means of bringing both disgrace upon themselves and dishonour upon their employers by their censurable and unworthy conduct . . . you have seen one in the highest walks of society, a noble lord, an unoffending master, murdered in the dead of night, in his own house, in his own bed, by the hand of his own servant – and a servant, who from the peculiar character of his employment may be considered as having received in special trust the person and the property of his employer, for he was his personal attendant. . . . And everything in his apprehension, in his conviction, in his confession, and in his disgraceful exit, reads a lesson of warning and instruction to us all; but more particularly to those who occupy the same sphere of life with himself.'

One can visualize the poor scullery maids quailing on the hard benches before the fiery preacher! Mr E. J. Miller, of Dover, who sent the author the *Penny Pulpit* copy of the sermon, handed down to him by his mother, adds: 'She spoke with devotion about the family by whom she had been employed, and she knew all the ramifications of the Royal family throughout Europe. At the same time she had a sharp tongue about anything that offended against her nonconformist conscience, and unhesitatingly consigned the Duke of Clarence and his brother the Prince of Wales to the flames of hell.'

At least in the chapels servants were not made to feel their inferior status. Mrs Lansom, of Portland, tells in a letter how, as a maid-of-all-work, she looked forward to Sundays: 'I joined a young women's Bible class at a Baptist church in the town and made many friends. Also on Monday evenings there was Christian Endeavour, which I joined and became an active member. Later I felt the call to become a Sunday school teacher. No one will ever know the joy I experienced in that community. . . . Had it not been for that fellowship I would never have been able to stand the strain of the "daily round, the common task." Incidentally, no one ever looked down upon my lowly estate, though the whole church must have been aware that by "profession" I was a maid-of-all-work.'

The last great evangelical revival in England was marked by the founding of the Salvation Army. And this, too, had its influence among the domestic servant class. Mr E. W. E. Booth, of Westbourne, Bournemouth, remembers a maid called Daisy at his parents' home in North London before the 1914–18 war: 'She used to attend the local Salvation Army citadel in Crouch Hill. In fact, she was so impressed that she sat on the "penitent form." One night she took me – at four years old – but never again! I remember the drums beating, but not the fact that a woman Salvationist came round selling the *War Cry*. I yelled out: "That's *Ally Sloper*" – a comic paper of the time. I was called a child of Belial. Daisy always came home from these meetings in an extremely bad temper – so much so that Mother remarked that Daisy "had been saved again". . . .'

It is more than likely that the promise of a better life in the world to come was all that many poor, lonely drudges had to sustain them. And when they had departed this vale of tears, *some* were remembered with a headstone on their graves. Mr Arthur J. Munby, the same Victorian gentleman we met in Chapter Three who married his servant in secret, devoted some of his time to collecting the epitaphs of domestics, which he published in 1891 in a book called *Faithful Servants*.

The inscription on the tombstone of John Quinny, fifty-six years in service at Tilsworth, Bedfordshire, ends: '. . . his master left him an annuity of £8.' Grateful employers remembered in chiselled stone Elizabeth Gay:

> who after a service of
> 40 years
> finding her strength diminished
> with unparalleled disinterestedness
> requested that her wages might
> be proportionately lessened.

The tombstone on her grave does not, alas, tell us whether the offer was accepted.

For the many who lived and died 'in service' there was one widely used epitaph that seems to sum it all up:

WELL DONE, THOU GOOD AND FAITHFUL SERVANT:
THOU HAST BEEN FAITHFUL OVER A FEW THINGS,
I WILL MAKE THEE RULER OVER MANY THINGS:
ENTER THOU INTO THE JOY OF THY LORD.

5

HIERARCHY BELOW STAIRS

His Lordship may compel us to be equal
upstairs, but there will never be equality in
the servants' hall.
(*Crichton the butler in*
The Admirable Crichton.)

It would be quite wrong to assume that it was only the employers who believed in class distinction. The servants themselves were extremely rank conscious and jealously guarded their positions in the hierarchy below stairs. Indeed the pecking order among servants was probably more complex than anything found in the higher reaches of society.

A servant in a good position was inclined to be haughty towards his inferiors, which he often interpreted as including his master's inferiors as well. In 1883, under the heading 'Reflected Glory,' the cartoonist George du Maurier depicted a shopman calling out to a footman: 'Here! Hi! Are you His Grace the Duke of Bayswater?' The magnificent flunkey replies in all seriousness: 'I HAM!' And, of course, at the very peak of domestic service Queen Victoria's faithful ghillie John Brown was hated and feared by many a gentleman of rank at court whom he treated with scant respect.

A search was being made one day at Balmoral by one of the servants for a lady who was staying there. John Brown pointed to the end of the corridor and said: 'There's the woman you want,' in a voice loud enough for the lady to hear. She complained to the Queen that she'd been insulted by being called a *woman*, but this only brought the answer: 'Well, but after all, wasn't he right? What else are you and I but women?'

This plain-speaking Highlander never bothered with ceremony. On one occasion he expressed his disapproval of the Queen's dress by asking: 'What's this you've got on the day?' When he died Victoria wrote: 'His loss to me (ill and helpless as I was at the time from an accident) is irreparable, for he deservedly possessed my entire confidence; and to say that he is daily, nay hourly, missed by me, whose lifelong gratitude he won with his constant care, attention and devotion, is but a feeble expression of the truth.

> A truer, nobler, trustier heart
> More loyal and more loving, never beat
> Within a human breast.
> BALMORAL, NOVEMBER 1883.

From John Brown the grand order extended downwards to the humblest hall boy or page. In between were the serried ranks of stewards, housekeepers and butlers, ladies' maids and governesses, cooks, housemaids, footmen, coachmen, tweenies and scullery maids. The size of establishments varied, as we have seen already, from the domestic armies employed in ducal mansions and stately homes down to the lonely cook-general in the small suburban villa, a pathetic creature who had no one to order about or look down upon.

The servant hierarchy developed from the gangs of armed ruffians who constituted the domestic staffs of nobles and gentlemen in Tudor England, and formed the backbone of Henry VIII's armies in wartime. By the eighteenth century it had become 'the general plague of the nation' ... as one horrified Portuguese traveller in England in 1808 put it, adding that servants 'are not to be corrected, or even spoken to, but they immediately threaten to leave their service.'

A large complement of servants was a status symbol among the rapidly growing middle class, made prosperous by England's expanding trade overseas. Tobias Smollett remarked in 1797: 'About five and twenty years ago very few even of the most opulent citizens of London kept any equipage, or even any servants in livery ... At present every trader in any degree of credit, every broker and attorney, maintains a couple of footmen, a coachman and a postillion.'

The nobility were obliged to increase their domestic staffs to meet this challenge from the new rich mills and the colonial trade. According to E. P. Thomson's *The Making of the English Working Class*, 'Next to the agricultural workers, the largest single group of working people during the whole period of the Industrial Revolution were the domestic servants.' As far as their standards of living, food and dress was concerned they were better off than any others. They quickly divided themselves into 'upper' and 'lower' classes.

In James Townley's *High Life Below Stairs* (1775), the Duke's servant says: 'What wretches are ordinary servants that go on in the same vulgar Track ev'ry day! Eating, working and sleeping! But we, who have the Honour to serve the Nobility, are of another Species. We are above the common Forms, have Servants to wait upon us, and are as lazy and luxurious as our Masters.'

Thus a distinct line of demarcation was drawn between upper and lower domestics, and between the servants of the nobility and gentry and those of the mercantile classes. In large establishments, upper and lower servants dined separately. Upper menservants wore ordinary clothes, while their subordinates were dressed in livery, or uniform.

At the top of the hierarchy stood the land steward, who managed the estate, collected rents, settled disputes between tenants and so on. A house steward or housekeeper ruled supreme over the indoor servants. Immediately beneath him were two servants of equal rank, gentleman-in-waiting and master of horse, the former as personal attendant and confidential adviser to the master and the latter in charge of the stables and all the outdoor livery servants, from coachmen down to stable boys. But by the first quarter of the eighteenth century both these posts had nearly disappeared, to be replaced by those of valet and clerk of the stables. Below them, in the ranks of upper servants, came the butler and gardener.

Of the inferior menservants – those who wore livery – the coachman ranked the highest. Under him came the footmen, grooms, under-butlers, under-coachmen, park-keepers and game-keepers, and lowest of all the yard boys, hall boys and foot boys, sometimes as young as eight or nine years old.

Footmen were the peacocks among domestics, with their plush breeches, silk stockings and powdered hair, which survived as ceremonial attire for footmen up to the 1930s. As J. J. Hecht comments in *The Domestic Servant Class in Eighteenth Century England*: 'Their livery emphasized their remoteness from productive labour. The footman's routine exposed him to view more consistently than did that of any of the others.

'He was in consequence, one of the most vital parts of his

THE MODEL MAID OF ALL WORK

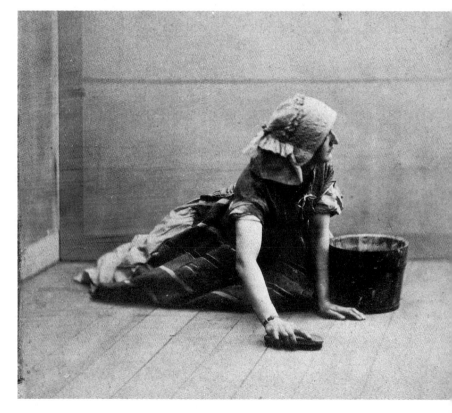

Far left: Seven o'clock in the morning – making up fire. Thought to be Hannah Cullwick, general servant at Kilburn, *c.* 1860, photograph from the Munby Collection

Centre: Hannah Cullwick washing – Munby Collection

Left: Hannah Cullwick carrying tray – Munby Collection

Below left: Hannah Cullwick scrubbing – Munby Collection

Carrying water, *c.* 1902

A Victorian maidservant in a private house, c. 1860

Cook

Coronation party in Chelsea
Town Hall

School for maids

Engravings from George Cruikshank: *Let them ring* and *It's my cousin, ma'am* from *The Greatest Plague in Life*

CADBURY'S COCOA
FOR BREAKFAST

RY'S COCOA AS A SUBSTITUTE FOR MILK.—"The excess of fatty matter has been carefully eliminated, and thus a compound remains which conveys in a ilk a maximum amount of nutriment. We strongly recommend it as a diet for children."—*Medical Mirror.* Cadbury's Cocoa contains all the elements indispensable for and development of the body for children and adults. It is delicious, nutritious, stimulating, digestible, comforting, and a refined beverage suitable for all seasons, all all occasions.

Advertisement for Cadbury's cocoa from *The Graphic*, 1886

Advertisement for Brooke's Monkey Brand soap, 1908

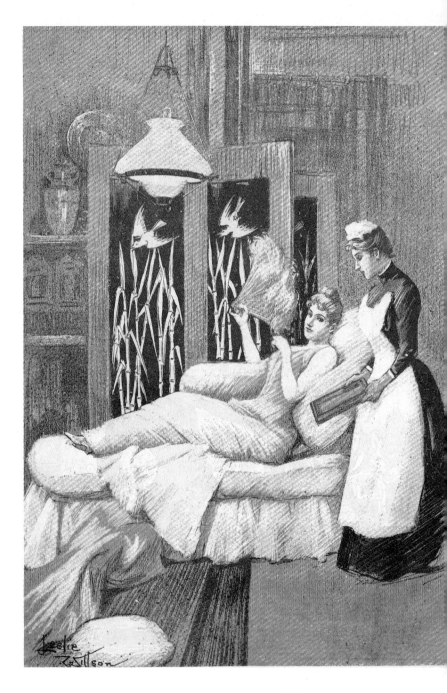

WHAT'S IN A NAME, 1892
Mistress: Didn't the gentleman leave his name?
Maid: Yes, ma'am; he said it was Immaterial

master's equipment of display. Large establishments usually included a considerable corps of such servitors.' During the eighteenth century, footmen, in their liveries of silver, scarlet and emerald green, were often used to make formal calls known as 'How de'ye's,' paying their employers' respects to friends, inquiring after their health and so on. Ladies of fashion also liked to have a black boy or two, sumptuously attired in silks, lace and satin, in their retinue.

The footmen also had some outdoor duties of a more functional kind. They carried flambeaux whenever their masters had to walk the unlit London streets after dark. There was a species known as a running footman, a special mark of his employer's importance and superior rank. He was usually dressed in a black cap, jockey's coat and white linen trousers. His job was to run alongside his master's carriage and carry a six foot long pole, which served many purposes: to test the depth of the puddles in the road, to stop horses if necessary and even to beat off highwaymen if there was an ambush. He often had a small sword or cutlass hidden in his clothing as additional armament.

When trains ousted carriages as long distance transport the footman lost this glamorous outdoor role and became little more than an ornamental flunkey normally employed indoors waiting at table and answering the door to callers.

Women servants had no ornamental function and were kept out of sight as much as possible, attending to the routine and menial functions. Primacy among the females below stairs belonged to the lady's maid, the personal attendant of the lady of the house. In the eighteenth century it was common for young girls to be placed with milliners and mantua makers, either as apprentices or as paid assistants, to equip them for situations as ladies' maids.

Next in rank to the lady's maid was the housekeeper, serving under the steward if there was one. If not, she supervised the whole establishment. Lowest of the female upper servants was the cook.

The chambermaid headed the lower female servants, who included housemaids, laundry maids, dairy maids and maids-of-all-work. At the bottom of the scale was the lowly scullery maid who cleaned the kitchen, scrubbed the pots and pans and did most of the servile work.

There were the strictest rules governing the divisions between all these various categories and the means of stepping up from one to the next, and the grand order survived throughout the nineteenth century and well into the twentieth.

John Gorst, who was a footman to the Duke of Portland at Welbeck Abbey at the turn of the century, gives us a picture of the hierarchy in that grand establishment. The upper servants were called the 'Upper Ten,' comprising the steward, the wine butler, the under-butler, the groom of chambers (whose main function was to look after the furniture in the great house), the duke's valet, the housekeeper, head housemaid and ladies' maids. The lower servants, who for some inexplicable reason completely unconnected with their numbers were known as the 'Lower Five,' were never allowed to mix socially with the upper servants except at the annual Christmas ball for the domestic staff.

The Upper Ten took their meals separately in the steward's dining room, waited upon by the steward's room footman. The Lower Five ate their meals in the servants' hall, served by the hall porter and the hall boys.

The Upper Ten had white wine and claret with their meals, while the Lower Five had only beer. The Upper Ten used fine china and glassware at their table. Their napkins, neatly rolled in silver rings, were changed every day. The women wore dress blouses and the men smoking jackets to late supper. Visiting ladies' maids and valets were expected to dress similarly.

The superiority of the Upper Ten over the rest of the servants was taken very seriously indeed by everyone concerned because the duke always promoted from within. Every young servant in the house could aspire to a place at the steward's room table, and his own napkin neatly folded in a silver ring. Mr Gorst, in his book *Of Carriages and Kings*, writes: 'At Welbeck the upper servants adopted an arrogant attitude towards the under servants. Mr Clancy, the wine butler, was the haughtiest and most pompous of them all.'

There was a vast difference between service in this sort of establishment and that in the middle class homes employing no more than three or four servants, usually all female. A typical five-storey house in South Kensington in the early 1900s employed only three: what was called a 'dinner party cook,' a house parlourmaid and a tweeny, who did all the rough work and was usually recruited from an orphanage at the age of thirteen.

As the twentieth century progressed and servants became more expensive and more difficult to find, even the homes of the aristocracy had to cut down on the numbers employed. By 1928 the Earl of Londesborough was making do with only thirteen servants at Blankney Hall in Lincolnshire: butler, footman, steward's room boy, odd man, valet, head housekeeper, first, second, third and fourth housemaids, cook, kitchen maid and scullery maid.

Mr Bentinck, who was the steward's room boy, wrote to me from Mears Ashby Hall, where he is still in service, and described the hierarchy of those days: 'Cook did not go into the servants' hall. She had her own room off the kitchen and was waited on by the kitchenmaid, who also had to cook breakfast for other servants and lay out all cook's utensils, as well as firing the kitchen ranges. The steward's room boy had to clean the butler's shoes and press his clothes and put his white bow on for dinner. No one except the housekeeper, who sat at one end of the servants' hall table and the butler at the other end, were allowed to speak at meals. The butler had to be addressed as "Sir" and the housekeeper as "Madam" and the rest of the staff spoke only when spoken to, and this rule applied, too, when they met the gentry.'

The experience of Mr Bentinck – 'in gentleman's service all my working days' – conforms to the general custom. Young servants always had to address their seniors as 'Sir' and 'Madam'. There was a strict etiquette about such matters below stairs. Cooks and housekeepers were always 'Mrs', whether married or not. Ladies' maids, secretaries and governesses had to be given the title of 'Miss' by those below them.

In the larger houses the upper servants commonly had a room of their own, separate from the servants' hall and referred to as a 'Pug's Parlour.' They either dined separately from the servants in the servants' hall or at least retired there for sweet, cheese and coffee.

Where they all dined together at the same table they were seated according to precedence, and grace was said by the most senior. In a letter to the author from Odiham, Mr Ivor Taylor recalls: 'When the butler put his knife and fork down that was the signal for *everyone* to do the same, so God help if you were a slow eater. A woman used to come in and scrub the long passages, and at table the butler would say to her: 'What will you have, Mrs McDonald?' She'd reply: 'I'll have a little bit of each, Mister. I never misses anything.' The butler on returning to the pantry used to say to the first footman: "That awful woman. So bad for the under-servants, too!". . . .'

By the later years of Victoria's reign there had been gradual changes in the balance of power below stairs. The number of menservants had declined, the ranks of women grew stronger and the influence of their key members grew apace.

In middle class households, the parlourmaid, prettily attired in black alpaca and white lace, with long streamers flowing from her neat little cap, did the jobs done by the more formal footmen in the houses of the aristocracy. The cook/housekeeper with her white starched blouse and apron, a large bunch of keys dangling at her side as a badge of office, was a figure to be reckoned with. Mrs Blanche Hall, a former scullery maid, writes from Southport: 'When she walked along the corridors you could hear the swish of her skirts and jangling keys. I used to tremble.'

A dishonest cook or housekeeper had ample scope for cheating because she gave orders to tradesmen and kept the books. She controlled the stores, the still room and the linen cupboard. Nothing was bought or disposed of without her knowledge. Most ladies only inspected the books once a week and any self-respecting cook expected advance notice if the mistress intended to descend to the kitchen.

The Victorian cook held total sway over the kitchen staff. Many were tyrants and it was not unknown for an entire household, staff and employers alike, to be utterly terrified of a domineering cook. Mrs Beatrice Gardner, of West London, recalls one she served at the age of fourteen who required the kitchen range to be polished with a piece of black velvet to obtain the exact gloss so necessary to her culinary art. In a letter to the author, Mrs Gardner writes: 'I used to run and hide in the coalhouse if I upset any milk or gravy. Her rage had to be seen to be believed.'

The jealousy and snobbery among the female upper staff was almost unbelievable. Parlourmaids felt it was beneath their dignity to speak to or acknowledge anyone in the kitchen. But occasionally there was humour. Mrs Gardner writes: 'I well remember having to carry cans of hot water up many flights of stairs when her ladyship was changing for dinner, and being met en route by one of the housemaids who, with a straight face, told me I must also take a certain china article (used in the days of no bathrooms) and hand this to her lady in her room, together with the can of hot water. This I duly did, and to my utter dismay, received a month's notice for being "rude and insolent," which was really funny when I think how terrified I was to even speak to anyone. But of course no one knew it was the fault of this wretched housemaid, playing a trick on a child who had just left home.'

When she became a nursemaid, she had to accompany old nanny and the children to the seaside for a month at Weston-super-Mare. She remembers nanny heading the daily procession to the beach with the best pram and the newest arrival in the family, while she, being only a nursemaid and of inferior rank, had to walk a suitable distance behind with a rather old pram and the more troublesome young members of the family. In the nursery the children were beaten by nanny for the most trivial offences and no one dared to intervene.

Mrs Gardner continues: 'When I became a fully-fledged nanny I must have been the world's worst. I must admit to letting the little ones do *nearly* everything they wanted to, as long as it made them happy. But I got some very nice people to "nanny" for and although I have two grown-up children of my own, several of the people I worked for still keep in contact with me . . . a dear family with whom I was connected for nearly forty years have recently died out, leaving me to feel very sad at their loss, they were as dear to me almost as my own family.'

The nice nanny has become a part of our social history, but there were plenty of nasty ones, too. Mrs O. Scard, who worked as a nursery maid under an elderly spinster nanny writes to the author: 'She repeatedly informed me that I was there to wait on her and the two children hand and foot.' On days that nanny went out she had to wait up to warm her milk on her return. Miss Burbery of Merstham, who was a nursemaid, writes that nursemaids had to wait at all times on the nannies. Nannies never washed a cup or picked anything up from the floor. And nursery maids were not allowed to mix with the other maids in the house.

Miss Queenie Cox, whom the author interviewed at a flat near Victoria Station in London where she is still in service, worked as a fourteen-year-old housemaid in the same house as her older sister, who was nurse to the four children, and she was not allowed to have any contact with her: 'One morning I called my sister by her christian name and the lady of the house, who was an utter snob, corrected me: "*Nurse*, please!" If I saw my sister out with the children she was not allowed to speak to me, or me to her. Nurses were on a higher level, you see.' Another of the author's correspondents writes that the nurse who used to look after the small daughter of the medical officer at Aldershot Barracks in the early

1900s actually had a batman to wait on her, polish the pram and escort her when she took the child for a walk.

Governesses, who were neither servants nor part of the family, were much resented below stairs. They taught the daughters of the aristocracy and the upper middle class at home. In 1851 there were over 20,000 of them in England but they had little or no prestige in society. Mrs Blenkinsop in *Vanity Fair* explains why they are despised by the other servants: 'I don't trust them governesses, Pinner. They give themselves the hairs and hupstarts of ladies, and their wages is no better than you nor me.'

An advertisement in *The Times* in 1856 illustrates what Mrs Blenkinsop means. It is from a governess offering her services 'to instruct and attend to young children, and if occasion, to assist the lady in domestic affairs. Is quite competent to teach reading and writing, and is very proficient at piano and singing, and willing to do anything not menial.'

Plain, dull girls were said to be fit only to work as governesses. They lived drab, lonely lives in their schoolrooms at the top of the house. Charlotte Brontë was one, and she wrote of one of her employers: 'I have never had five minutes' conversation with her since I came, except when she was scolding me.' When the small son of the family said to her in front of his mother: 'I love 'ou, Miss Brontë,' the mother exclaimed in tones of surprise, if not shock: 'Love the *governess*, my dear!'

Governesses began to die out as a class towards the end of Queen Victoria's reign. As the twentieth century advanced, and with it the part played by the young English lady in many aspects of life hitherto closed to her in the professions and even in commerce, the governess became virtually redundant. Like their brothers, the daughters of middle class families were being sent away to school.

Like governesses, ladies' maids were often disliked by the lower servants because they appeared to put on 'airs and graces.'

In fact ladies' maids had to be well-spoken and very discreet, like a good secretary. They were all too easily suspected – from above and below stairs at the same time – of carrying tales or gossip. In return for being intelligent, cheerful, capable and willing to turn their hands to hairdressing, needlework and anything else milady required, they were given their own room, and a lower maid to clean it for them. The most sought-after ladies' maids were often French.

But it must be admitted that ladies' maids were very ready to complain about anything which seemed to encroach on their dignity, their 'position.' They strongly disliked, for instance, being expected to work for more than one lady in a family. Ladies encouraged them by not having the slightest idea where their things were kept, by possessing dresses that buttoned up the back, and by being incapable of putting on their shoes or drawing the blinds.

An anonymous late-Victorian work entitled *The Lady's Maid* warned them against getting above themselves: 'I trust you will bear constantly in mind that your elevation into comfort and luxury – your better clothes, your seat in the dressing room and on your master's carriage are only circumstances in your service and not given to you to last. Your heart should still be where your station is – among the poor; so that if you have to return to your old ways of living when your years of service are over you may not feel hurt or degraded but as if you were returning home.'

No lady wanted an elderly maid as a personal attendant. If the lady's maid failed to catch a husband while she was still in the bloom of youth her future was bleak. And as Jonathan Swift had pointed out to her kind a century earlier, she had to guard against becoming the prey of milord, or the eldest son or one of the upper menservants, unless they wanted to marry her.

In the below-stairs hierarchy, everyone had to be aware of his or her place: 'I was promoted from scullery maid to kitchen maid and that meant the lady's maid could say good morning to me before the scullery maid.' (Mrs Reynolds, London, in a letter to the author.)

And how much petty nastiness there was in the servant hierarchy! A housemaid cook who spent fifty years in service writes to the author: 'I've had one or two bad mistresses but most of the nastiness was caused by the maids themselves. There was always a lot of jealousy among the upper staff. I preferred to work where there were four in staff as I found a more friendly atmosphere than in larger households. If only three maids were kept, two would probably pal up together and leave the third one out. I also preferred to work with the upper class rather than the middle class. This was not snobbery as I found the upper class treated one much better even though the wages were usually lower, the upper class being noted for being tight-fisted.'

Amidst all this feminine clawing and spitting, one class of male

71

servant kept his position through the Victorian era and even improved his status: the butler. As we have seen, in the eighteenth century he rated at the foot of the upper servants' table, below the valet (who like the lady's maid was mistrusted by most servants for being too close to 'them upstairs') and the clerk of stables. He emerges at the turn of the century as *the* dominant figure in domestic service, a leader of men – and all those women below stairs, too.

He was an imposing figure who, when answering the door, could distinguish at a glance between gentlefolk and 'persons.' As E. S. Turner puts it in *What the Butler Saw*: 'As often as not, he was kept for ostentation and sometimes for intimidation. He was expected to be deferential to his superiors and haughty towards his inferiors, which included his master's inferiors.'

Butlers, like cooks and housekeepers, were sometimes guilty of over-indulgence in strong drink (John Brown, the 'butler' in the household of Queen Victoria herself, erred in that direction), but this was a failing which could be overlooked in view of their splendid bearing. Butlers were not hired like mere servitors: in their own words they 'engaged themselves,' an expression they felt to be more dignified and in keeping with their station in life. They were rarely youthful and their devotion to duty was such that they often remained as bachelors.

Arthur Inch was literally born into service, for his father was a butler too (between 1890 and 1934).

Mr Inch recalled the life of a butler as told to him by his father. It was a hard life in some ways: his father never had a lot of time off and never had a holiday. But once a butler Mr Inch's father did little actual work, and no dirty or hard work at all. His main function was admirably summed up 'by Williams' in a little hand-book handed down to Mr Inch by his father: 'Like the footman, the butler has to perform many duties in small families not generally considered as belonging to his position in large establishments. But in all establishments it is his duty to rule. In large establishments more particulary, this exercise of judicious power will be greatly required; for under servants are never even comfortable, much less happy, under lax management. . . .'

This then, was the hierarchy below stairs. Much of it depended on upper servants' estimations of themselves and their 'positions.' In 1848 the *Observer* told the story of a butler who was deeply affronted when his master ordered him to go into the kitchen and squeeze some lemons. When he pointed out, politely, that this was a job for an inferior servant, his master gave him a shove so that his tray and glasses fell to the floor. When he was asked to clear up the mess he refused, again on the grounds that this was work for a menial. By this time the master, convinced that his butler was mad or drunk, or possibly both together, had lost patience entirely. The butler was given his wages and told to leave.

The butler, attempting to sue his former employer, later told the magistrate at Marlborough Street: 'I do assure your worship, I was obliged to carry my portmanteau and carpet bag myself for upwards of half a mile!' The magistrate, however, remained unimpressed and ruled that the original order to squeeze lemons was not unreasonable, even when the butler (playing his ace card, presumably) pointed out to the bench: 'But it was to make *punch*.'

Clearly, the magistrate knew nothing of the other world below stairs, and the newspaper records that the butler left court with the air of a deeply injured man.

6

LIVING AT THE TOP, AND WORKING AT THE BOTTOM

As we saw in Chapter 1, the Victorian house was designed to accommodate two distinct and quite separate classes under the same roof. The householder's family lived on the ground, the first and possibly the second floor. Their servants lived and ate in the basement and slept in the attic. This seemed to all concerned, at the time, a wholly practicable and sensible arrangement.

The problem of how the servants were to commute between attic and basement without disturbing 'the family' was solved by having two sets of stairs. The back stairs, uncarpeted and unlit, were for the servants. The two worlds under one roof were divided by a door, white paint and crystal knob on one side, green baize and gunmetal knob on the other.

To enable those who belonged 'upstairs' to summon those 'downstairs' when they wanted something done, the house was fitted out with a complex network of bells, with push buttons or cords in all the rooms used by the family and a box with indicators down in the basement to show the precise location of the bell that was being rung. 'Ring for service' meant exactly what it said in those days, and woe betide the maid or footman who failed to answer promptly.

The word 'stairs' figures prominently in the mythology of domestic service – Upstairs and Downstairs, Below Stairs, and so on – and it figures prominently in the recollections of the former maidservants and boys who had to stagger up and down them laden with scuttles of coal for the fires which warmed all the family rooms (even the bedrooms), cans of hot water for baths (in the days before bathrooms were commonplace fixtures) and the inevitable 'slops'. There could be as many as a hundred and fifty steps from the basement to the attic of one of those tall Victorian town houses, and there were no lifts.

Mrs Chambers, in a letter from Plymouth, recalls one such house she served in: 'There were eighty stairs from top to bottom, sixteen stairs to answer the front door, thirty-two stairs to the drawing room with tea.' As a footman at Londonderry House, Arthur Inch once put on a pedometer and in the course of a long and busy day during 'The Season' when big parties were the custom, he recorded eighteen miles without once leaving the house.

Attics had been favoured as quarters for servants from the eighteenth century, or at least for the lower orders – valets and ladies' maid sometimes had rooms adjoining their masters and mistresses to be more readily on call, stables and coach-houses often had quarters for grooms above them, while on country estates, gardeners or even butlers had cottages in the grounds.

Memories of those dismal cells at the top of the house are still vivid among survivors of the domestic servant class. They slept two, three or even four to a room, in some cases sharing beds. When gas, and later electricity, were installed many employers regarded the extra expense of extending gaspipes or power cables up to the attic unjustified, so the maids continued to 'go up at night with their candles' and rose shivering on bitter winter mornings when ice had formed on the water in the jug and the face flannels were frozen solid.

They remember, in letter after letter, the grey distempered walls of their rooms, the bare floorboards, the lumpy flock mattresses on iron bedsteads, the spotted mirrors and chipped washbasins, the ill-assorted oddments of furniture relegated from the family's rooms to the servants' quarters, and, of course, the chamber pots and the wash-stands.

As late as the 1920s and 1930s, when domestic service as a way of life was dying out, this was still the pattern in the home of titled people in a fashionable part of London, Cambridge Gate, Regent's Park: 'The wash-stands were rather drab wooden affairs with the usual jug, basin, soap dish and toothbrush holder. And these were 'hand-downs' from the best bedrooms when an article was broken, so that the servants' "sets" never matched.' (Doris Hazel, tweeny.)

'One room I occupied in London at the home of a judge was very sparsely furnished with an iron bed, a chest of drawers and a wash-stand, not even a strip of carpet to step on. A lot of maids' rooms just contained the junk from the other parts of the house.' (Lady's maid, 1925.)

'I shared a bare-boarded room with the kitchen maid, quite separate from the other nine staff. A single iron bedstead with a lumpy mattress, a large chest of drawers and spotted glass, wash-stand, jug and basin and chamber pot – considered to be well furnished.' (Scullery maid, 1924.)

The only thing that these garrets had in common with the other bedrooms was the view from the window, perhaps rolling park-land, an orchard or a well-kept garden, and the scents from the flowers and the songs of the birds. Otherwise they might just as well have been in the meanest slum.

But some servants would have regarded a room in an attic, however small and sparsely furnished, as a privilege. A young girl in service in a boarding house in Canterbury, just before the 1914–18 war, had to sleep in the *bathroom* on a folding bed: 'When I got up in the morning I had to fold my bed up and put it on the landing in time for the "paying guests" to have their bath. I had no cupboard or chest of drawers to put my clothes in – I hung my coat and dress on the bathroom door and my other clothes were kept in the tin trunk that no servant girl was ever without.' (Violet Turner, of Faversham, in a letter to the author.)

The lower menservants in quite aristocratic establishments were often expected to sleep in folding cots in the basement, to segregate them from the maids sleeping at the top of the house. At 3 Grosvenor Square, the London house of the Duke of Portland, the hall boys slept on cots in the servants' hall in the basement and waited on the lower servants. They hardly ever left the basement or saw the light of day. Lack of fresh air, cramped quarters and bad ventilation gave indoor servants a pale-faced, anaemic appear-ance. A footman who served in a private house recalls in a letter to the author that the bed in the butler's pantry folded up into a cupboard during the day and at night came down across the door of the safe where the silver was kept, so that his sleep had a bonus for the employer by ensuring that his valuables were guarded throughout the night without having to pay a watchman.

An Army major, who started out as a hall boy in 1930, says in a letter to the author: 'My bed was in a cupboard in the servants' hall and could only be let down at night after the other servants had finished their evening meal and had decided they had finished with the room for the night. Heaven knows where I would have laid my head if I had been ill. There were no inside sanitary arrangements below stairs and after the doors were locked and barred for the night, the hall boy was forced to use a chamber pot which was emptied by the junior housemaid every morning very early. Likewise, I had to be up at dawn to make up my bed and strap it down in order that it could be pushed into a vertical position and shut up in the cupboard before I laid the table for the servants' breakfast.'

Not all servants' accommodation was as shabby as this. More than thirty years earlier, footmen at Welbeck Abbey, seat of the Duke of Portland, had comfortable rooms with coal fires to warm them and they shared a large bathroom known as the 'Powder Room' because there, before the wide mirrors, they dusted their hair with 'violet powder' as part of their flunkey attire. There was a menservants' billiard room in which no women were allowed – indeed, the maids' corridor was called the Virgins' Wing and was presided over by a prim head housemaid.

But English homes, even the grandest of them, were notoriously backward in such matters as modern plumbing, sanitation and central heating, which for years were regarded as new-fangled American nonsense. Not many saw anything wrong in the time-honoured method of heating water on a coal-fired range in the kitchen and carrying it up several flights of stairs in large brass cans. A big kitchen range could easily burn a hundredweight of coal in a day, but coal was relatively cheap (£1 a ton in 1899) and who cared if all those fires upstairs and downstairs made the fogs in London even thicker? Fogs, like hip baths and baths shaped like vast metal coffins, were part of the English way of life.

There were some progressives, like Mrs Ruth Sherren's grandfather, a Harley Street surgeon, who devised his own shower bath. She tells the author that it was a somewhat Heath Robinson affair utilizing a large tank, which required the services of a footman with a stepladder to fill it. When the distinguished doctor was ready for his douche, the flunkey on the ladder at the command 'Go!' pulled a chain – and down came the water.

Even when the bathrooms came in, gradually, with the twentieth century, it was utterly unthinkable that servants should use the same ones as the family. If there was no second bathroom, they were despatched to the wash-house to bath in the water which had been used to boil the sheets and the linen. While gentlefolk bathed once a day, a bath once a week was considered quite enough for a servant, to be taken on a day off. 'In 1918 servants were not allowed to use the bathrooms, though there were two, one for the lady and gentleman and one for the son. We had a tin bath in our bedroom which was in the attic and we had a lot of stairs to take our hot water up.' (Mrs Farrant, of Sevenoaks, in a letter to the author.)

Where a servants' bathroom *was* provided it was a very different affair from those of the family, with their beautifully tiled walls and floors, thick towels, gleaming brass taps, glass shelves, vanity mirrors and elegant arrays of essences, bath salts and perfumes. The servants had an old iron bath, rough and yellowed inside, squatting nakedly on bandy legs. The wash basin might have a flowered pattern, once fashionable, but if so it was almost certainly chipped or cracked and a 'cast-off'. If there was a mirror it would be pock-marked and chipped, too, and the towels would be thin and well worn.

Doris Hazell, writing of the 1930s in a letter to the author, says: 'We were each allowed one bath a week and allocated different days and times which had to be religiously kept. The menservants always had their bath in the afternoon when all the female staff were downstairs. Of course there was a washbasin in the best bathroom, so no wash-stands were needed except in the servants' rooms. There was no washbasin in our bathroom, merely a stone sink and an enamel bowl where we did our personal washing which we hung on enormous clothes racks attached to the ceiling and lowered by ropes on a pulley. Woe betide anyone caught in the bathroom out of hours! The menservants were kept quite apart from the women. Whereas our bedrooms were in the attic, theirs were right down in the basement and when I made their beds and cleaned the rooms the rule was that the door must be kept open and the butler kept a wary eye from the pantry door to make doubly sure there was no "hanky-panky" going on.'

Segregation of the sexes, segregation of the classes . . . it seems a quaint survival in the 1930s of the old Victorian order, but Doris Hazell experienced it herself. Segregation was even extended to the 'smallest room in the house' when that became part of the domestic arrangements. As early as 1854 an advertisement in *The Times* extols "the comfort of a fixed water closet for £1, in the garden' – surely a somewhat dubious luxury on a cold, foggy mid-Victorian night.

When, with the march of progress, 'toilets' came indoors, the servants' 'privies' stayed outside in the cold. In one house, fondly recalled in a letter to the author, the servants' lavatory even had a name, 'Ivy Cottage', because it was reached by a covered way concealed by thick ivy – 'The children of the house were forbidden to use it and regarded "Ivy Cottage" with a certain amount of awe. . . .'

So we come to the basement – the 'engine room' and the workshop of Victorian households, and of the homes that valiantly maintained the traditions of domestic service for decades after Queen Victoria was in her grave. The basement was reached separately from the main part of the house, down a flight of steps leading to the servants' and tradesmen's entrance. Suburban villas with no basements, but aspirations to better things, tried to maintain the tradition by having a side entrance marked 'Tradesmen only'. The only light that filtered into the basement where the servants lived and worked came from the 'area', fenced off from the street with wrought-iron railings.

The kitchen was to be found down here, the source of what one household management book described as 'the calm comfort of our English homes.' The kitchen was large, with a stone-flagged floor and a black 'Eagle' cooking range. It had a coal grate with ovens either side of the fire, a hot water tank and many concentric rings which could be lifted out to make a place exposed to the fire according to the size of saucepan in use. The heat could be adjusted by using 'dampers' which controlled the air draught to the blaze.

A passage led from the kitchen to the larder, cool and dank, with a brick floor and slate shelves. This would have pheasants hanging and large perforated zinc covers to ward off the flies from the meat, butter and other perishable foods. Refrigerators were a long time replacing the old-fashioned larder.

There was coconut matting to ease the chill of the stone floors in the kitchen, a large, heavy kitchen table, wooden kitchen chairs and, if the kitchen was also the servants' sitting room, perhaps a few basket chairs with cushions and a huge dresser with a drawer for each of the maids' personal things, knitting, books and so on. All the heavier washing up was done in big wooden sinks in the scullery, while knives and silver were cleaned in the butler's pantry.

There would be a dark coal cellar going underneath the pavement with a hole for tipping coal down a chute, covered when not being used with an iron lid. Other below stairs 'offices' might well include a still room and other store rooms, a wine cellar, a wash house, a boot house and maybe a housekeeper's room. These dark, dank cellars were often infested with beetles and cockroaches, mice and rats, to terrorize young serving maids when they came down in the mornings to light the fires and scrub the floors.

But when all the staff were about they were cheerful enough places. Doris Hazell, again: 'All our meals were served in the servants' hall, the window of which looked out into the area, so dark that the electric light was on almost all day . . . our food was good and plentiful. As far too much food was always served in the dining room upstairs, we quite often had cold chicken, grouse or pheasant, or the cold joints left from lunch. This "upstairs" food was always served to us at supper time – our dinners (mid-day meals) were always hot and cooked especially for us. The breakfasts were varied and hot except for Sunday mornings when it was always a plate of ham. Of course, the cook always prepared the ham herself and a very good cook she was, too. There was a very strict observance of each servant's position around the table and each one was served in rigid order. The butler carved and sent the plates down to cook, who served the vegetables and back would come each plate to its rightful place. The tweeny was served last and my mouth watered for ages at that table, passing plate after plate until my own landed in front of me. All the youngsters had enormous appetites, most of us had come from very poor homes indeed and every meal was a feast to us.

'There were never any special foods bought for the staff, margarine was unheard of, the pastry was all butter and we revelled in it. "That's *real* gentry for you," the old housekeeper used to tell us, "no meanness in the kitchen here – like some of your 'get-rich-quick' merchants who think the servants can do a good day's work on stale bread and margarine and left-overs from *their* table.' She was quite right, too, as I discovered when I left three years later to "better" myself by becoming a housemaid in Kensington.'

Abundance of food is something many former servants remember with nostalgia – not surprising in view of the poor diets of many working class families at the time. These are the memories of people in service who are alive today in the era of deep-freeze, 'convenience foods' and stuff out of plastic packets. Indeed, up to the 1939–45 war, when that way of life died, tinned foods were little used except in bed-sitters, and cooks made everything themselves, concocting their own sauces, using fresh vegetables and game sent from the country – rabbits, hares, pheasants, grouse, snipe, woodcock and wild duck. Pheasants were hung until they were 'high': stories of maggots crawling up their arms as the birds were prepared for cooking are part of the folk-lore of former kitchen maids. Stilton cheese was covered with a napkin soaked in stout and left until it was crawling with cheese mites. Cooks baked their own bread and made their own jams.

But not all servants shared such gastronomic delights, even as left-overs. Neither, it must be admitted, would most of them have wanted to. Even so, the middle class theory that servants 'preferred' plain food was sometimes used as an excuse for pinching and scraping on the household budget at their expense. A fourteen-year-old girl in service in a chemist's house in 1914 existed on the following sparse diet:

Breakfast: four slices of bread and dripping, two cups of tea.
Dinner: quite a good two-course dinner.
Tea: small pot of tea, three slices of bread and margarine.

On Sundays she was allowed, in addition, a piece of cake and a cup of cocoa at bedtime.

And from another letter: 'I had to carry up our evening meal to the nursery, which included only one sweet and that was for Nanny. I never could understand why I was not allowed a sweet or how Nanny could eat it all and never share.' (Former nursery maid, 1930.)

A lady's maid in the early 1900s remembers that: 'The food was not very plentiful and everything had to be carefully used. I never had an egg all the time I was there. Breakfast was fried bacon and boiled, alternately. On Sundays we had either sausages or bloaters. The joint that was bought for the dining room used to last the servants' hall for the rest of the week. We usually had it cold with hot vegetables until it finally appeared as a sort of hash which nobody wanted. Tea was bread and butter and a small cake, gooseberry jam one week, and plum the next. We did get occasional treats after dinner parties; anything that wouldn't keep, like ices, we demolished. My employers were well off and only mixed with "the County". The reason the food was so sparse was my lady's fault. She had a good housekeeping allowance but she was so fond of clothes some of it got wangled to pay for them.'

Careful employers had store cupboards which they kept locked, doling out weekly rations of tea, sugar, jam, butter and so on to the staff. A great fuss was made if the amounts apportioned to each member of the staff failed to last the week and an eagle eye was kept on every candle and every cake of soap. In some houses servants were allowed only margarine, never butter.

Mrs Edith Bodden, who became mayor of the Lancashire town of Eccles in later life, started work as a general servant in 1900. Her second 'situation' was at Malvern, working for an old lady and her companion. In a letter to the author Mrs Bodden says: 'The larder in the house was locked until the mistress came down each morning. Eggs were twenty for a shilling but the maid was not allowed one every morning and the silver had to be taken upstairs and left at the foot of the mistress's bed each night.'

Miss Chubb writes from Devon: 'Where I was in service the under staff had half a pound of butter per week, kept in individual saucers in quarter-pound pats in a safe beside the servants' hall. This was ample as it was only eaten at tea-time because all the other meals were cooked.'

It must be allowed that however poor the accommodation of some servants, and however meagre their rations, they were still probably better off than they would have been at home in days of dire poverty. On the other hand, in their homes they would not have been able to compare standards with those who were better off. In service they could see 'how the other half lived' and it is clear that some of them, at least, resented it.

A housemaid making her mistress's comfortable feather bed could compare it with her own lumpy flock mattress. As her feet sank into the thick pile of the carpet in the drawing room she could hardly fail to notice the difference between that and the bare boards, or the thin strip of threadbare rug in her own room.

For in their own small way, the middle classes of the period were just as avid seekers after elegance and style in their lives as were the aristocracy: the gong for dinner, the evening ritual of whisky and sherry decanters, letters brought in from the hall on a silver tray, tea with the best china, complete with crumpets. Apart from a carriage, the most sought after status symbols in the middle class home were a piano and a harp.

The more intelligent and perceptive of the servants, witnessing all this *style* at close quarters, no doubt wished to be a part of it and bitterly resented being treated always as an entirely separate kind of human being. Of course, very many did 'improve' themselves just by proximity to a better way of life than the one they had been born into, and it stood them in good stead long after they had left domestic service.

As Doris Hazell puts it: 'It was a hard life at times but a solid foundation of all sorts of knowledge that you could draw on in married life to the advantage of your whole family. What shop girl, out of the slums as I was, could know how to handle cutlery in a select West End hotel? Who could choose a meal from a French menu and know what wines were suitable for each course? Who could cook those same meals for special celebrations at home? Or darn linen so that the darns were almost invisible? Who else of our class would know how to address an earl, bishops, even royalty – or enjoy a box at a West End theatre? Even an appreciation of paintings, fine furniture and china comes in useful up the Portobello Road! I had the run of a fine library for three months of the year so I'm much more widely read than most of my acquaintances, too.'

No, of all servants the one most to be pitied was the single-handed maid in a lower middle class household, who hadn't even the consolation of seeing the grand life at second-hand. She lived a life of unremitting drudgery, made worse by almost total isolation from her own kind. It is not difficult to imagine the loneliness of a young girl of thirteen or fourteen, taken from the unceasing clamour and chatter of a large family and placed in a situation where she was alone for most of the time. These 'cook-generals', the general dogsbodies of the suburbs, were expected to live in the kitchen as if it were really a servants' hall.

There was no outlet for the youthful high spirits of girls like this. One of the author's correspondents has written with great sympathy and insight of a maid-of-all-work employed at the turn of the twentieth century in her parents' home when there were seven young children to be looked after: 'She was fifteen when she arrived and already had her hair "pinned up", which in that era meant she was grown up. She was a big, strong girl and she needed to be, as a good deal of hard work was expected of her. . . . On the few evenings when this poor girl had no work to do she would sit in a dimly lit kitchen and knit horrible cotton lace with which she trimmed her calico underwear. Sometimes she would write a letter home and come into the living room to ask my mother if she might "slip down to the box". Fancy having to ask permission to post a letter. This "slipping down to the box" often took some time, I imagine this lonely creature met and talked to boys. How she must have longed for people of her own to talk to! Once a month she went home for the day. She only lived about four miles away and I think she was able to get a horse bus part of the way. . . .'

Such girls sometimes stayed with the same family for years, growing old before their time, to become 'treasures' called Ethel or Daisy, neat in cap and apron. Others came and went and were quickly forgotten by the family they served, or at best dimly remembered. Some were simply 'unsuitable' and 'had to go'. But well-bred people made a point of never being rude to their servants. If obliged to get rid of them they would always say: 'I'm afraid we shall have to let you go,' rather than tell the girl outright she was dismissed, and they would always try to give the girl as good a reference as they honestly could.

In retrospect, it seems a pity that so few of these otherwise kind and likeable people took any account of the aspirations and human feelings of their servants. The outlook of a charming lady, in a *Punch* cartoon of 1898, showing a benevolent old gentleman where the housemaid sleeps, seems representative of all too many employers. The old gentleman says: 'Dear me! Isn't it very damp.' The lady replies: 'Oh, it's not too damp for a servant.'

In 1905 *The Lancet* declared that servants' quarters were often abominable enough to warrant the attention of the local authorities' medical officers of health. Six years later a bill to 'regulate the hours of work, mealtimes and accommodation of domestic servants, and to provide for periodical inspection of their kitchens and sleeping quarters,' was drafted. But that was as far as it got. It was never printed.

7

FIRES BEFORE BREAKFAST

Work, work, work,
Like the engine that works by steam!
A mere machine of iron and wood
That toils for Mammon's sake—
Without a brain to ponder and craze
Or a heart to feel and break.
            (From 'The Song of a Shirt.')

These lines from a Victorian ballad were written in sympathy with
the apprentice dressmakers who slaved from 5 a.m. to midnight,
or later, during the London 'Season' when gowns in which young
ladies would be presented to the Queen had to be finished on time.
But the words apply just as well to their sisters 'out at service.'
Indeed, although the Factories Act of 1891 limited the hours of
work for women to twelve a day, with one and half hours for
meals, the new laws did not apply to domestic servants, who
continued to work longer hours every day until well into the
twentieth century.

In 1842 public opinion had been aroused by a Royal Commission's report on the appalling conditions in which women and
children were forced to work in the mines, and this led to laws
removing all women and *children under ten* from employment
underground. But, fond as the Victorians were of Commissions of
Inquiry, they never ordered one to inquire into the conditions of
service in their own homes. Mistresses deplored the fact that shop
girls were kept on their feet for fourteen hours a day, and quite
ignored the fact that their own servants were sometimes on duty
for as many as *eighteen* hours.

For most of the year, the servants' working day began and
ended by candlelight, starting at five or six o'clock in the morning

when they lit the fires before breakfast and finishing when the warming pans had been placed in the beds and the master and mistress had retired for the night. *All* servants had to be early-risers, and Miss Chubb, in a letter to the author from Devon, says that the people who employed her as a tweeny in 1909 ensured that their staff rose on time by having a chiming clock on the landing below their sleeping quarters which was kept a quarter of an hour fast. During the 'Season' bedtime for the servants was often midnight or later, but they were still expected to get up at the usual time in the morning to light the fires.

In the mid-Victorian period servants had no recognized time off at all except to go to church – when they went into service they sold to their masters *all* their time 'except what God and Nature require to be reserved.' But by the 1890s employers had bowed to liberalizing pressures to the extent that they gave *one day off a month*. It was known as 'cook's day out.'

By the early 1900s, thanks to the insatiable demands of those ungrateful wretches below stairs, many servants were being given one afternoon and evening off *every week*, as well as time off on Sunday. There was no set rule about it, the time off varied from district to district, even from street to street, depending on the inclinations of the employer and militancy of the staff. Even by the 1920s some downtrodden 'generals,' working on their own with no one to make common cause with, were never allowed out except once a week from 4 p.m. to 8.30 p.m.

But after the 1914–18 war some 'advanced' ladies started giving their maids a whole day every month, in addition to an afternoon and evening every week. The majority of employers however, considered such treatment 'soft' and letting the side down.

Days out were never given as a right. A half-day started at 3 p.m. after the maid's work had been thoroughly done and luncheon served upstairs and cleared away. The following story told to the author by a Harrogate woman took place in the 1920s: One afternoon, a maid who had on her outdoor clothes ready to go and enjoy her weekly spell of freedom which ended at 9 p.m. was stopped by the mistress, who said she hadn't seen her take down the slip mats that morning. When the girl confessed that, owing to lack of time, this chore had in fact been omitted, she was sent back upstairs to change into cap and apron, take up all the mats and carry them down to the backyard for their daily beating. After that, with a telling off for her 'wicked ways,' she was allowed to change and have a belated half-day.

Punctuality in returning from time off was a mania with most employers, understandably in the case of young girls for whom they were responsible. But even middle-aged maids had to be back at 10 p.m. promptly and failure to comply was simply not tolerated. Miss Doris Bodger, who went into service in a Stately Home at the age of thirteen, tells the author that she was allowed out after her work was done but had to be back at 7.30 p.m., or 8.30 p.m. as she became older: 'So sometimes we only had about two-and-a-half hours off a week.'

An Englishman's home was a place where he did as he pleased, so his demands on his servants were unpredictable and irregular. Even in the afternoons, when in theory there was little for them to do, the servants had to be on hand to answer the summons of the bell upstairs. The heaviest work-load was in the mornings and at night when late dinner had to be cooked and served. The prosperous *bourgeoisie* in the northern mill towns preferred 'high tea' but among the upper classes, and therefore among the aspiring middle class, formal dinner was *de rigueur*. Working class people, including servants, had *their* 'dinner' in the middle of the day and their meal in the evening was called supper.

Between the main course and the sweet the parlourmaid would go round the table with a silver crumb tray and brush to remove all traces of the bread which was always crumbled on to the damask tablecloth. Before the dessert she handed round finger bowls into which the guests dipped their sticky fingers.

It was a strict point of etiquette that dishes must be handed to the left side of the diner, never to the right. And one unfortunate parlourmaid in the London house where Mrs Margaret Wyllie lived as a child (circa 1914) committed the unforgivable crime of passing round the port in an *anti*-clockwise direction. The mistress murmured: 'The *other* way please, Allen.' (Parlourmaids, in deference to their position, were always addressed by their surnames, not by their christian names as the lower maids were.) Mrs Wyllie writes: 'Allen, who had an Irish temper and was incensed by criticism in public, banged the decanter down on the table with a violent crash and marched out, slamming the door behind her. Although she had been with us for as long as I could remember, and I was sad to part with "Lizzie" as I called her when out of Mother's earshot, she was dismissed the next morning.'

Domestic work in the days when there were no labour-saving aids was arduous, demanding and fatiguing, as well as monotonous. While the supply of domestic labour was still plentiful, few labour saving devices were introduced into English homes. Why waste money on machines, when servants were there to do the work? There were no vacuum cleaners or washing machines, no patent detergents, rubber gloves or 'gentle' washing up liquids.

Acres of stone-flagged floors and miles of corridors had to be scrubbed by hand and carpets had to be brushed from a kneeling position after dried tea leaves had been scattered into the pile. The task was made doubly difficult by the fact that Victorian homes were cluttered with countless ornaments and bric-à-brac which had to be dusted every day.

Also, servants had to make their own cleaning materials – silver sand and vinegar for scouring copper pots, melted beeswax and turpentine for polishing the floors, furniture polish from linseed oil, methylated spirit, turpentine and white wax, blacking from ivory black, treacle, oil, small beer and sulphuric acid. They even made their own tooth-powder from bole armoniac, bark, camphor and powdered myrrh.

One petty trick employed as a 'test' of a servant's diligence and honesty was to hide coins under the carpets or in the loose covers. If the maid failed to find them she was skimping her work. If the coins disappeared and she said nothing, she was dishonest!

There were oil lamps to be cleaned, trimmed and filled and candlesticks to be attended to. Some of the author's correspondents recall those country rectories, huge places with as many as eighteen bedrooms, that even in the 1920s were still lit by lamps and candles because electricity had not yet come to the village. Lamps were filled and cleaned in the 'lamp room' below stairs. Even piped water was considered a luxury in some country places – one maid was found sobbing in the pantry with water flooding out of the butler's sink because she didn't know how to turn off the tap. She had never seen a tap before in her life.

Housemaids were continuously on their 'poor feet' up and down the stairs day and night, scurrying around with scuttles of coal, cans of hot water and laden trays – answering the incessant jangle of the bell. Some maids were hardly ever seen standing up; they were always on their knees, and in strict Victorian households they had to cover their feet with their long skirts in case anyone *saw their ankles*.

Washday, like every other day, was arduous, with tub and 'posser', rubbing board, scrubbing brush and big iron mangles with heavy wooden rollers. Mistresses were *particular* about the washing: as one household book advised: 'If you observe iron moulds on the linen, speak at once to the laundry maid. It is possible she throws the washing cloths on a *brick floor*, which will cause iron mould as soon as rusty iron does.' The ironing was always finished before the maid went to bed that night. There were no electric irons, the ironing was done with flat irons heated on the hob. And there was a great deal of starching to be done – caps, aprons, antimacassars, pillow cases and so on.

For those households which could not boast a resident laundry maid there was a whole army of washerwomen ready to do the job for a couple of shillings and a bit of bread and cheese, or the left-overs from the dining room table. In the 1850s 'respectable laundresses' by the dozen advertised their services in *The Times*. Each claimed to have 'good drying grounds, a plentiful supply of water, clever French ironers and every convenience for getting up linen in a superior manner.' Mrs Hoare, laundress, of 61 Bayham Street, Camden Town, even boasted her 'own horse and cart.'

Boys who started in service under the various titles of page, house boy, hall boy, footboy or steward room boy were hard-worked, too, as Arthur Larke, who went into service in 1911 at the age of twelve, recalls. He had to polish the boots and pipe-clay the tennis shoes, and the cutlery had to be scoured every day on a knife board, using an abrasive called Wellington Knife Powder. When knife-cleaning machines (one of the first labour-saving devices in English homes) were introduced, many employers, including Arthur Larke's, refused to buy them on the grounds that they 'blunted the knives.' Mr Larke also had to pluck a dozen or so pairs of poultry each week, sent in from the home farm – chickens, ducks and game in season. He writes: 'The chickens were usually alive with fleas and so would I be by the time I had finished. But the fleas would die at sunset.'

So it went on, the never-ending grind of daily domestic life: 'The only thing that seemed to matter was work. The cook, a Methodist, would quote pieces of scripture to me as "Cleanliness comes next to Godliness" and "Whatsoever thy Hand findeth to do, do it with all thy Might." Even the old grey parrot would shout out: "Do your work!" ' (Ellen Russell, South Ealing, in a letter to the author recalling domestic service in 1918.)

Mrs Wavell, of Kentish Town, a tweeny at thirteen, started her working day at 5 a.m., and at 9 a.m., after breakfast, filed into the morning room for prayers at the end of a long line of servants all in strict order of seniority. As they left, each had to take a tiny scroll from a cardboard box held out to them by the master. They were 'God's promises', meant to carry them through the long working day. On her first morning as a tweeny, Mrs Wavell remembers hers read: 'Come unto me all ye that are weary and I will give you rest.'

There was little enough rest for servants. Even between duties there was always mending or darning to be done for the 'family'. The rules governing the conduct of their labours were strict, as Mrs Edith Bodden, writing to the author, remembers from her days as a parlourmaid in the early 1900s: 'When making the beds I had to put sheets round the valances in order that my clothes would not come into contact with the bed clothes. I have seen the kitchen maid scrubbing the kitchen floor at 9.30 p.m. and as for myself I had to be in the dining room at 7 p.m. All food was handed to me through the serving hatch and I had to stay until dessert was on the table, approximately 1½ hours. If I didn't stand perfectly still when the family were eating I was brought before the mistress the following morning and chastised.'

Many employers made a habit of drawing up detailed work schedules for each of their servants, so that there could be no misunderstandings about what was required of them. Mr Williams, of Wilmslow, sent the author a copy of those drawn up for a parlourmaid and housemaid in a Somerset village between 1905 and 1925, a period when their duties changed very little. The house had been built by his maternal grandfather in 1860 and there was no electricity supply to the village until 1934.

PARLOURMAID
to be downstairs at 6.30 a.m. Summer
6.45 a.m. Winter.
Open shutters first.
Do dining room fire, and dust room.
Lay breakfast by 8.15 a.m.
Dust Hall and Stairs, Morning Room and Drawing Room.
After own breakfast clear Dining Room breakfast.
Help make beds. Make own bed.
Mondays: Trim Lamps. Help given with cleaning lamp chimneys. Wash glass and silver. Clean Drawing Room and grate. Lay fire.

Tuesdays: Clean Dining Room silver. Afternoon: own day off.

Wednesdays: 1st week – clean Dining Room.

2nd week – clean Hall, and polish brass and oak.

3rd week – clean extra silver.

Thursdays: Clean and polish silver.

Fridays: Clean Parlourmaid's Pantry.

Saturdays: Clean Morning Room and China Pantry. Dust Stairs and Dining Room after lunch.

Sundays: Light Drawing Room fire if needed. Alternate Sundays: get afternoon tea and wash up. Lay supper table. Time off after 6 p.m. or 2 p.m. on alternate Sundays.

Generally: Answer front door. Wait at meals, clear and wash up. Bring in coal and logs, as needed.

To be in by 10 p.m. on days off

HOUSEMAID

To be downstairs at 6.30 a.m. Summer

6.45 a.m. Winter.

7.30 Make and take tea to Miss Ada and Miss Ethel. Later take visitors' tea and hot water to bedrooms. Open spare room windows. Clean best shoes. Polish Nursery floor. Dust Nursery, Billiard Room and back stairs. Empty slops, Top Landing. Make own bed.

After 8.15. Strip beds and empty slops. Clean bath and basin and dust Bathroom. Help downstairs only when Dining Room is cleaned, except when Billiard Room grate has to be done.

8.45 Kitchen breakfast, Make beds each morning.

Mondays: Before breakfast, soiled linen to be listed in Nursery. All bedrooms dusted, Bathroom floor polished and taps cleaned. Trim lamps – three bedrooms and other upstairs lamps – and clean lamp chimneys. Clean brass water cans. Own washing, clothes, etc., stockings, handkerchiefs every other week.

Tuesdays: 1st week – Miss Ada's bedroom cleaned.

2nd week – Miss Ethel's bedroom cleaned.

3rd week – a spare bedroom cleaned.

Get tea and dinner.

Wednesdays: 1st week – Dining Room cleaned.

2nd week – clean bedroom silver.

3rd week – clean a spare bedroom, windows and brass cans.

Afternoon: ironing.

Thursdays: 1st week – clean own bedroom, except when any other room needs cleaning – such as Billiard Room or any spare bedroom.

2nd week: list linen for laundry. Put clean linen in airing cupboard. Clean cork bath mat and can cupboard.

3rd week – ditto.

Afternoon – own day out.

Fridays: Clean both landings and three staircases.

1st week – clean stair rods and brasses.

2nd week – clean landing windows.

3rd week – polish landing floors and lavatories.

Saturdays: General dust. Clean goloshes. Scrub floor of Housemaid's room.

Sundays: Help downstairs after breakfast. Slight dust to bedrooms in use. Help Parlourmaid wash up and wait at mid-day dinner. Alternate Sundays: get afternoon tea. Lay supper table. Time off after 10 p.m. or 2 p.m. on alternate Sundays.

Generally: Help wait at table whenever needed. Help wash up evenings when there are more than six to dinner. See all luggage taken to and from bedrooms, and unpack if needed. Afternoons: Sewing till 7 o'clock except when required to help wait and wash up, then own time after that. 4.20 p.m. Get kitchen tea and wash up. Trim candle lamps every morning. Vacuum landing carpets each morning except when a big room is being cleaned.

To be in by 10 p.m. on days off.

One can see how the comfortable middle class home was run according to Milton's phrase 'Order is Heaven's first law'. Books such as *The Footman and Butler – their duties and how to Perform them* (by Williams) told servants how to carry out every task, from making a bed to washing up the dinner things, from filling a warming pan ('sprinkle a little salt over the hot embers before using'), to testing a really fine ham. Everything had to follow a procedure. Even preparing a hip bath for the housekeeper had to be done according to a certain system, as Miss Doris Bodger describes in a letter to the author: 'I had to lay a large blanket on her bedroom floor and put a three-fold screen around it. Then I carried in a large can of cold water and another of boiling water, laid sponges and soap dishes on a stool and covered over the can of boiling water with a bath towel and a bath rug. When the housekeeper had had her bath I had to bale out the water into a bucket and carry it along to the housemaids' cupboard for emptying. The hip bath was then cleaned with Monkey Brand soap and stood up in an alcove behind the screen, while the towels and blankets were hung up on a line in the housemaids' pantry.' (Miss Bodger refers to *c.* 1913.)

Fires were a tremendous chore in every house, great and small. A house employing eight servants might burn half a ton of coal in a day, and Dorothy Hill, writing from Torquay, tells me that during a cold winter she shifted three tons of coal in one week, keeping fires roaring in the drawing room, dining room, study and all the bedrooms.

Before gas or electric cookers were introduced all the cooking, and heating of water, too, was done by the coal-fired range in the kitchen. This black monster had to be cleaned and lit by 6 a.m. and the cinders sifted to be used later in the day for building up the fire. The range itself was blackleaded every morning and the steel fenders and fire irons polished with emery paper and brickdust until they shone like silver. The hearth would be whitened by rubbing it with a special 'stone'. Flues had to be cleaned out once a week as they quickly became clogged with soot.

In winter all the other fires had to be lit before breakfast, too, the grates blackleaded and the fenders and fire irons polished. Fire-lighting is becoming a lost art, but in the 1890s and early 1900s that, too, was a subject for discourse in *Warne's Model Cookery* (circa 1890): 'If it is done badly the room will be filled with smoke, which is very injurious to furniture. It is well when first winter fires are commenced to hold a blazing paper up the chimney for a few minutes before the first fire is lighted. This will dispel the cold air in the chimney. . . .

'The fire is laid by first placing cinders, rather apart, at the bottom of the grate; then a piece of paper – *not* coarse brown, which will smoulder – and then a few crossbars of pieces of wood, which should be kept *well dried*; on the wood some rubbly coals – not too close together, for a draught is required to kindle the fuel . . . Light with a lucifer match – use Bryant and Mays, because theirs will *not* ignite unless they are rubbed on their own box, and thus they are less dangerous than those which will kindle by stepping on. . . .

'Some persons light fires with wheels made with resin and other combustible materials. They are useful, and perhaps cheaper than wood, but not very safe things in a house, as they easily ignite. The housemaid should be careful not to waste wood. A clever girl will light two fires, if the grates are not very large, with one good-size bundle. One wheel, value one farthing, will light a fire.'

Fire-lighting could be one of the maid's sorest trials, as Mabel Johnson recalls from her days in the house of an Eton school-master during the First World War: 'Sometimes the wood was green and wouldn't ignite. I used to weep with frustration at the delay, and fear my work would not be finished in time for break-fast . . . brasses to shine, stairways, doorsteps, carpets to sweep, floors to polish (mixing our own beeswax and turpentine) on our knees pushing a lighted candle ahead . . . no bathrooms at that time, I had to lug in hip baths and five gallon cans of hot water, brass cans which were kept shining with polish and elbow grease. . . .'

The only daily breath of fresh air that these slaves of the mop and bucket ever had, and the only time they saw the 'front' of the house, was in the early morning when they were required to clean the front steps. Doris Hazell remembers it in the 1930s in vivid detail. She writes: 'At 6 a.m. each morning I toiled up the area steps wearing my rough apron and carrying a cleaning box (containing metal polish, dusters and polishing brush) in one hand and a soft broom in the other. First I cleaned the brass on the front doors – letter boxes, keyhole, two enormous door handles, bell-pull and knocker. Then I swept the doorsteps and returned to the area door to reappear with a large bucket of nearly cold water, kneeling pad and block of hearthstone, and whitened the door-steps (the under housemaid having opened the front doors in my absence). On an icy cold, dark winter's morning, and half a gale blowing across Regent's Park it was not a job I enjoyed. I was not allowed to wear any kind of jacket either over or under my uniform, or we should "lose face" among the other servants in Cambridge Place, and my hands were always badly chapped and often bleeding in the winter. As they were constantly in water, doing the vegetables, washing up in the scullery, scrubbing the lino in the servants' hall, the brick-tiled floor of the kitchen and the rough stone passages in the basement, it was quite useless to try to heal them.

'After breakfast, back to the scrubbing brush again. The back stairs went from basement to attic, plain wood with no covering whatsoever, and I learned to know every inch of those stairs – where I could dash away at them and where I had to go more carefully because they were worn and splintered. The rubbers on all the servants' shoes made black marks, especially on the stair "risings" and those stairs used to be pure white when I had finished. I was given a handful of soda to put in the water and household soap which arrived from the Army & Navy Stores in bars about a foot long, a nasty mustard in colour and very harsh on my poor, broken-skinned hands. . . .'

But if the work of tweenies and scullery maids was heavy and rough, the lot of the 'general', working alone in a smaller house, was even harder because she had to combine their duties with those of cook, housemaid, parlourmaid and, if there were children in the family, nursemaid, too. She had to do everything from cleaning boots and emptying slops, to waiting at table, which meant hurriedly washing herself and putting on a clean apron.

Mrs Barnett, of Stockwell Park Road in South London, had experience of just such a situation as cook-general to an elderly couple in the 1920s. In a letter she describes how she used to rise at 6.30 a.m. to clean and light the kitchen range, and at seven take up tea to the master and mistress and raise all the blinds. By 8.30 sharp, when breakfast had to be on the table, she had cleaned and lit the dining room fire, polished the brass on the front door, dusted the dining room and laid the table, as well as cooked the breakfast.

She had to clean the master's boots and put them on him at 9 a.m., empty the spittoon, wash it out and leave a little water in it – 'One morning I dropped the beastly thing into the lavatory pan and broke it, to the great annoyance of the mistress who made me pay for it by stopping my wages of fifteen shillings a week. The new pan cost me £1 7s. 6d.'

On another occasion, while laying the breakfast table, she picked up the aspidistra (a much-loved plant for decoration in Victorian and Edwardian homes, which is now as extinct as domestic service), and in her own words it 'flew through the air,' smashing against the wall. Two weeks' wages were 'stopped' to pay for it.

In addition to her multifarious indoor duties, she was required to cut the lawn and roll it, and exercise the dog. In retrospect, it seems remarkable that some of these maids-of-all-work did not collapse from sheer exhaustion, but there was always *Warne's Model Cookery* at hand to give homely advice and encouragement: 'Recollect, my little general servant, that if your place is a hard one, it is also the best possible one for training you for a better. After all, too, you have not more to do, nor, in fact so much as you would have as the mistress of your own home when married, when you would probably have to clean house, work for your family's support, and take care of children, besides enduring anxiety and the many cares of the mother and wife.

'In your place you have no care for daily bread or clothes. Your food and raiment are sure, and you have every comfort. If you rise early, bustle about, and waste no spare moments, you will get through your work very well – only do *think* about it. A little arrangement and thought will give you Method and Habit, two fairies that will make the work disappear before a ready pair of hands. . . .'

There is much, much more in a similar vein. The well-intentioned ladies who wrote such books had little conception of what housework really meant, because even employers of a solitary general servant did little actual work themselves. They sometimes helped to make the beds, although it was pointed out that this was by no means their duty. The single-handed maid always had to answer the door to callers, snatching a clean apron from the kitchen drawer and leaving the pots in the sink to do so.

Apart from the never-ending round of firelighting and scrubbing away the grime that quickly accumulated from the smoke-laden air, a great deal of domestic work was concerned with looking after the large broods of children common in Victorian times. Although the nursery staff were not cooped up in the basement all day, their regime was just as demanding as that below stairs. As *Warne's Model Cookery* put it, their duties were very responsible ones as they had to watch over the 'health, safety and comfort of the little ones in the nursery'. The first duty was to keep the little ones clean: 'It is best, we think, to give them their bath *at night*. The water of the bath should be lukewarm (unless a cold bath is especially ordered). They may be *washed* in cold water in the morning. Brush the hair carefully and tenderly so as not to hurt the little heads'. The book emphasizes that the influence of the nurse for good or evil is *very great*. She should make sure that 'no word may meet young ears in the nursery that is unfit for them to hear.'

The nursery maid who served the nanny had to be up at 6.30 to clean the grate and light the nursery fire, make nanny's early morning tea and then clean and carry meals from the kitchen up the stairs to the nursery, wash up, wash and iron, clean the prams, take the children for afternoon walks, mend sheets and clothes – until, like her sister below stairs, she went exhausted to bed. When she had her time off it had to be a day that suited nanny and if nanny went out to tea with the children *she* was always left with a pile of mending to keep her busy until they got back.

In a letter to the author, a former nursery maid at a seven-storey Victorian house in Princes Gate in the early 1900s recalls having to go down to the kitchen at 11 p.m. to fetch a glass of hot milk for the head nurse. This was the last duty of a day which began by calling the nurse with her morning tea in bed at 7 a.m. The nursery maid always carried the baby up and down stairs and pushed the pram while the head nurse walked alongside. She also had to deal with everything that the baby put on, or took off. The small girls wore white pinafores trimmed with lace which had to be specially done after washing and drying with 'goffering' tongs which were heated to set the frills. Babies' bottles were strange contraptions with long rubber tubing and glass connections, which had to be cleaned with long wire brushes.

A great deal of servants' time and energy was taken up with the preparation of the mounds of food which the 'comfortable classes' consumed. As far as the kitchen was concerned those long dinners at night starting with soup, then fish, game meats, sweets and savouries meant hours of arduous preparation. 'I had often to put spinach through a sieve and raw chicken after it had been beaten in a pestle with a mortar. At first I cried and said: "I can't get it through." But I was soon told by cook: "There's no such word as can't." . . .' (Former kitchenmaid in letter to author.)

The elaborate meals created masses of washing up. The soot that coated saucepans, collected from being over the fire, had to be brushed off before they could be washed. Puddings were eaten much more than they are today and the suet clung to the cloths they were boiled in. They were the most horribly greasy objects to wash and as hot water did not come from a tap, it would usually get cold before the scullery maid had finished the washing up in her big wooden sink. Soda was put into the water to disperse the grease – and it roughened and reddened the maid's hands still more.

One girl who had to do this work at a large house in Hove in the early 1900s became ill with a very bad abscess. In a letter to the author, she recalls: 'The lady didn't know of it until I couldn't put a plate on the rack and had to go to the doctor. He couldn't believe I'd been working with an arm in such a dreadful condition.' In many houses servants were never expected to be ill, or even to feel ill. It was not until they dropped that anyone usually bothered to get them to bed and send for a doctor.

The author's mother, who worked as a kitchen maid at Denmark Hill in 1904, recalled that when she became ill the lady of the house sent for her own doctor to examine her. He found she was anaemic, perhaps not surprising in view of those long hours spent in a basement under artificial light. It was decided to send her to the family's country house near Maidstone in Kent for six months, because it was thought the fresh air and country food would do her good. But she was still expected to carry on working in the kitchens there, so she didn't get a great deal more fresh air than she had in London. However, to this day she still appreciates the lady's kind thoughts.

Some of the tasks servants were called upon to perform, particularly in the households of the upper classes, were bizarre, to say the least. When the Earl of Londesborough was steward of the Jockey Club and held a weekend party for his guests at Lincoln Races in the 1920s, the steward's room boy had to heat a poker with a small bowl on the end and walk with the butler from the ladies' corridor down the front stairs, while the butler poured drops of perfume into the hot cup. The object of this extraordinary exercise was to ensure that the ladies' walk downstairs to dinner from their rooms would be filled with fragrance!

Apart from *ironing The Times* when it was delivered in the morning, the housemaid was sometimes required to *stitch* the pages down the centre to keep them neat and tidy for the master in the evening. If these newspapers were for the lady of the house a little perfume might be ironed into the pages. (Information from Mr Arthur Inch.)

When the upper classes took to the moors to shoot birds in the autumn, lunch was taken out to them by their butlers and footmen. This sport created still more work for the servants, as Mrs Blanche Hall, a former scullery maid, recalls: 'I had to be down at 4.30 a.m. helping to cut sandwiches to send out for the beaters and preparing the elaborate lunches for the guests.'

And when the day's 'shoot' was over, there was still no rest below stairs. The staff had to count it, pluck it and hang it in the game larders where it would hang until it was crawling with maggots and ready to be prepared for the dinner table. And large parties were given in the evenings, so that the servants rarely got to bed before midnight.

Neither was there any respite for the servants who had been left behind at the London houses. The departure of the family to the country was invariably the signal for a thorough spring cleaning of the house from top to bottom. Carpets were taken up and curtains taken down. Wood-slatted venetian blinds were unstrung, scrubbed both sides, and strung up again. Furniture was washed all over with vinegar to clean off all the old polish and masses of beeswax and turpentine applied and rubbed until the wood was *warm* and the original lustre returned, while the poor maids' arms ached.

They had to stand on long ladders scrubbing away at the high ceilings with soda and water to remove the ingrained grime. White paintwork had to be scrubbed down and repolished with a special cream made up for the purpose. Scrollwork in wood and plaster, so beloved of Victorian interior decorators, was a trap for dirt and took hours of back-breaking work to clean.

Worn and torn sheets were brought out of the linen cupboards and turned 'sides to middle' to give another ten years or so wear, and any holes were darned exquisitely so that the mending was almost invisible.

The well-to-do revelled in fine things – heavy damask table-cloths and sheets that were embroidered and monogrammed – and their servants took an equal pride in caring for them. All those five-branched candlesticks, silver fruit bowls, flower baskets, finger bowls, wine stands and decanter holders were lovingly polished with Goddard's powder so that they graced the dinner table, gleaming in the candlelight.

In his pantry during long winter evenings, John Henry Inch, butler, devoted hours to cleaning his master's white leather hunting breeches, working to detailed instructions from Hammond & Co. of Oxford Street, who produced a special powder for the purpose. It had to be 'mixed with warm water to the consistency of cream' and applied with a sponge – 'if in possession of trees, the breeches should be placed on them to dry, taking care that the extreme bottom edge of the breeches comes down to the mark on the trees.' The immaculate turn-out of Lord Mountgarret when he rode to hounds as Master of the North Yorks Ainsty during the 1920s depended on these labours below stairs.

Such activities were time-consuming, in addition to the thousand and one other tasks which kept the large staffs of England's Stately Homes fully occupied. Miss Doris Bodger, who worked in them for fifty-eight years, starting as a tweeny at thirteen, wrote to me: 'There always seemed to be miles of corridors and some had to be pipe-clayed along the sides. Druggets – cover sheets – were placed over the carpets while this was being done. Some walls were lined with brocade instead of paper and this had to be brushed down with soft brushes, then rubbed over with tissue paper and finally with soft silk dusters. During spring cleaning, a linen drugget was hung along the picture rails and the floors were washed over before being polished with beeswax and turpentine, and when this was dried we had a huge lead-weighted polisher which was pushed back and forth while polish was applied.'

The result of all this effort was a glow and a lustre that 'made you feel as if you were looking into the heart of the wood'. When dances were held, the floors were sprinkled with french chalk and again the heavy leaden polisher was brought into play.

Those days have gone. No one will toil like that any more and, perhaps mercifully, the machines have taken over and made rough manual labour unnecessary. Yet, to many of the former servants who are still alive today, all that sweat over long hours, week in, week out, still seems worthwhile. As Miss Bodger puts it: 'When I visit some of the Stately Homes today, and see some of the beautiful furniture in such a lovely state of preservation, I often think how much the owners owe to we servants who took such a pride in our work.'

8

THE APRON WILL BE STARCHED

In matters of dress, the Victorians liked their servants to be easily, indeed instantly, recognizable as servants. A uniform for maid-servants developed during Queen Victoria's reign and lasted, with but minor modifications, chiefly in the length of the dress, up to the start of the Second World War. In the eighteenth century and the early part of the nineteenth, servant girls had no standardized uniform. They were expected to dress plainly in common working dresses, with quilted petticoats, worsted stockings and leather shoes. Servant girls who decked themselves out in silk gowns, fine gauze caps with lappets and streamers, flounced pettitcoats and long trains when they left the house were said to be 'fit only to act a play with strollers in a barn,' as the clergyman's wife phrased it in *The Servant's Friend*.

She tells her erring cook in this cautionary tale, published in 1824, 'Susan, I was quite astonished to see your dress yesterday, and must insist upon your not making such an appearance again, if you think of continuing in my house . . . you cannot dress too plain for me, as I told you when you first came, so pray let me see no more of your gew-gaws; common wages will not afford such things and they are quite out of character.' When the mistress had gone, Susan mocks her to the other servants: 'So I am too fine for Madam! Is she afraid I shall be taken for the Mistress?'

But although wenches who tried to get themselves up to look like ladies laid themselves open to the stern disapproval of the middle classes, lords and ladies often considered it a matter of personal prestige to have well-dressed servants. Servants in large houses in the eighteenth century were often given their em-ployers' cast-off clothes. Sometimes they were handed over as special rewards for good service, but more often it was done as a matter of course. When there was a death 'upstairs,' wardrobes of considerable size and fine quality were bequeathed to be divided among the servants.

The Victorians did not share these liberal attitudes. They were sticklers, like the rector's wife, for what was right and proper for servants to wear, as a nineteenth-century pamphlet published by the Society for Promoting Christian Knowledge made clear: 'You promised at your Confirmation to renounce or give up all the "pomps and vanities of this wicked world and all the sinful lusts of the flesh" . . . So, Mary Jane, be always well-dressed and thoroughly clean and respectable, but leave earrings, feathers, flounces and bright flowers alone.

'Remember St Paul's words to St Timothy about women dressing themselves in "modest apparel". While you are in service don't copy ladies. Wait until you have the same income and a home of your own.'

The double-standard that was evident in so much of what the Victorians said, and what they did, crops up again here. It is thought only right and proper that servants should be held to the confirmation vows, but it was acceptable for 'ladies' to go in for all the pomps and vanities, feathers and flounces, that they wanted. Such ladies would spend the equivalent of all their maids' wages for a year in a single outing to a dress shop.

Pious tracts such as *The Servant's Friend* instilled into servants that whatever fine clothes they put on, they would not look 'genteel' in them, because ladies had a manner, a way of carrying themselves, which a mere domestic could not hope to emulate. And, indeed, the majority of girls of that class and period would have felt most unhappy and uncomfortable if put into 'lady's clothes' and sat down to tea with the gentry in the drawing room. They knew their place, and were the better for it, according to many people.

But there were in the 1890s, some maids, particularly ladies' maids with 'ideas above their station', who liked to spend every penny they had on clothes and to walk out dressed in style. They were scornfully described by contemporary journals as 'abigails disguised like their betters,' and it was a widely held view that such young madams ended up as fallen women.

It was an attitude that persisted in the 1920s and the 1930s, when class distinctions in female dress were becoming more and more blurred, and when for the first time it was hard to tell the difference between a shop girl and a debutante from the way they dressed. Even then, as we saw in Chapter 3, servants were still being urged to equate silk underwear with sin. It was a proposition that undoubtedly made silk underwear all the more attractive to those poor girls who were forced to wear calico, or flannelette, next to their skin.

When permanent waving of hair came into vogue, servant girls who had 'perms' on their days out were also consigned to the flames of hell. Mrs O'Donnell, of Newcastle upon Tyne, who was a tweeny at a manor house in 1924, says in a letter to the author: 'I had my hair "shingled" and that made me the first in Newbiggin to have the new hair style. The mistress was horrified and told me she would have to think over whether she intended to keep me or not.' The threat in the last few words is, curiously enough, very similar to the one delivered by the rector's wife to the erring Susan in *The Servant's Friend* exactly a hundred years before.

Employers could not always dictate what their servants did outside their homes, but at least within them the rules of dress were strictly maintained. By the late nineteenth century the maid-servant's uniform was as recognizable up and down the country as that of a policewoman, a nurse or a traffic warden today. The maid had to have three sets of clothes packed in her little tin trunk when she went into service: cotton print dresses for mornings, black dresses with white caps and fancy aprons for afternoons, and her own outdoor clothes.

Miss Bodger, starting as a tweeny in a Stately Home in the early 1900s, remembers she had to have three or four print dresses, white bibbed aprons, a blue apron and a coarse hessian apron for scrubbing the stone passages in. For the afternoons she required a black alpaca dress, down to her ankles because legs were never seen. The dress had long sleeves and a high white stock collar.

The aprons for afternoon wear were large white muslin affairs with frills on the bands which went over the shoulders, and they were worn with large frilled mob-caps, some of which had long streamers down the back.

Employers were apt to forget that behind the starched uniforms there were people with human feelings like their own. The uniform assumed such importance in the order of things that it became a nation-wide standard practice at Christmas time to present the maid with a length of print dress material, usually in a ghastly shade of pink, or blue, with which to renew her uniform –

to be made up at her own expense. This present to servants was given regularly every Christmas by employers, almost without exception, as if it was laid down in some charter of domestic service to which they all subscribed. How the practice came to be so universally accepted remains shrouded in mystery.

In fact, maids resented the fact that *they* had to pay for their uniforms while most menservants were provided with theirs by their employers. In the 1890s the *Girls' Own Annual* published articles under titles such as 'A Young Servant's Outfit and What to Buy for it,' giving detailed advice on how to purchase an entire outfit for the first year in domestic service for £3 11s. 4¾d.

It is important to realize that in the 1890s this sum represented anything up to six months' wages for a tweeny. The girl going into service either had to work in a factory, earning perhaps 2s. 6d. [12½p] a week for *two years*, to save enough to buy the necessary outfit, or her family, relations and kind friends and neighbours could scrape together enough to buy it for her, in which case she was expected to repay the money in monthly instalments out of her meagre wages.

Letters from hundreds of former maidservants received by the author testify to the real hardship caused by the practice of girls' having to pay for their own uniforms before they could get a 'situation' in domestic service.

Mrs Holywell, of Basingstoke, who started work as a scullery maid in 1915 writes: 'I had print dresses, caps and aprons from my two older sisters cut down to fit me and second-hand underclothes in an old tin box. The only two new things I had were a black costume for which mother paid fifteen shillings [75p] and a new black bonnet with velvet ribbon at 5s. 6d. [27½p] which I had to wear to church on Sundays.'

She had to send her mother 10s. [50p.] from her monthly wage of 13s. 4d. [approximately 67p] to pay for the costume and bonnet. In those days there was a primitive form of hire-purchase operated by 'packmen' who called from door to door and provident societies. Mrs Holywell adds: 'At Christmas the lady gave me a length of material to have made up, which cost me 3s. 9d. that I could hardly afford.'

In addition to caps and aprons, maids had to provide themselves with stockings, which cost 4½d. [about 2p] a pair, and were darned and darned again and again to make them last. The long corridors and endless flights of stairs were hard on stockings and footwear, another recurring expense. The high button boots of Victorian maids gave way in the twentieth century to house slippers or light indoor 'ward' shoes with flat heels, rubber soles and a single strap buttoning at the side. They cost 2s. 11d. [almost 15p] a pair.

'I've always had to provide my own outfit. This would be about six white aprons and "Sister Dora" caps, two print dresses and sometimes a black dress for afternoons, though as a cook I didn't often wear the black dress. I made my own outfit. In the 1920s the underwear was made of unbleached calico which was cheap. When new it is very rough, but with a few boils it would go soft and white, and anyway it was all we could afford in those days. I knitted my own stockings, which were black, both for indoor and outdoor. I also had to have two aprons made of coarse "harding", a sort of sackcloth, for the rough work.' (A servant still in service after fifty years, in a letter to the author.)

Mrs Garner, of Leicester, tells how her mother took her to a house in 1914 where, as a girl of fourteen, she was to start in service. The mistress said the girl would have to have her hair in a bun, 'So mother took a few pins out of her own hair and did mine up for me.' The lady bought the standard uniform: black dress for afternoons, print dress for mornings, cap and white apron. Mrs Garner adds: 'The dress was so long I thought it looked dreadful. I cried every day for a week.'

Many servants were required to wear a special uniform when they went to church. Servants at 'the Hall' in country villages had an outdoor uniform of dark grey coats or cloaks, black Salvation Army style bonnets, black gloves, black shoes and black stockings. 'Black, always black, everything black. We were never allowed to wear coloured clothes.' (Third housemaid in a Lincolnshire country house, 1913, in a letter to the author.)

An ex-parlourmaid, in a letter to the author, remembers how she got out of wearing the hated black bonnet to church by cutting all the trimmings off it, so that it was unwearable. She then had to wear her own hat: 'Servant girls were not supposed to go out wearing hats of their own in case they were mistaken for the "young ladies" of the house.'

One does not have to be a mathematician to see what little was left to spare for buying fripperies to wear on afternoons off (assuming the servant was allowed to wear 'fripperies'). It is surprising when one looks at the few photographs available of servant girls in their outdoor clothes, how neat and charming they appear when released from the bondage of cap and apron. The photographs do not of course show the red, work-roughened hands that were the permanent badge of their calling. Good clothes were relatively expensive, so a servant was in any case limited by her pocket in her choice of outdoor clothes.

In Swan & Edgar's 'Great Autumn Sale', in 1899, a hundred chiffon blouses lined with silk were being offered at £1 1s. 6d. each [£1.7½] – 'usual price' £2.2s. [2.10]. Other bargains were 750 handsome embroidered robes, skirt shaped and seamed ready for lining, and embroidered material for the bodice at 15s. 11d. [almost 80p!] each, opera coats and circular cloaks, trimmed with fur and lined with silk, at two guineas [£2.10] instead of the usual three [£3.15], Paris model gowns, coats and skirts usually costing as much as seven guineas [£7.35] at half price, and '150 only Moretto Petticoats, black ground with coloured stripes, or all black' for 10s. 11d. [less than 55p].

Ponting Brothers, of Kensington, had decided to give 1s. of every cash purchase or cash order during their Winter Sale to the 'Kipling Poem Fund', to be devoted to the wives and children of men called to arms in the Boer War. *Their* bargains included a hundred dozen lace lappet scarves at 6¾d. [about 3p] each, four-button French suede gloves at 1s. 11¾d. [about 10p] a pair, ladies' flannelette shirts at 1s. 6½d. [about 7½p] each, and 'perfect-shaped corsets' for as little as 2s. 9¾d. [about 13–14p].

Clearly, the majority of these enticing items were beyond the reach of most tweenies even at bargain basement prices, but the lady's maid was able to dress like her mistress, because she often received most of her lady's beautifully cut clothes after about a year's wear. For travelling, she was sometimes given a dark coat and skirt, but more often one of her lady's former costumes.

The lady's maid never wore an apron, except perhaps a *tiny* muslin one if she were washing her lady's hair, and her shoes were cleaned downstairs by the scullery maid or the boot boy. One correspondent recalls that a French maid in a middle class home in the early 1900s, an expert needlewoman who made clothes for herself, the daughter of the house and some of the mistresses, usually wore a 'little beribboned black alpaca apron indoors. . . .'

Lady's maids were not expected to ape their mistresses in their dress and they were *not* above the rules governing servants' dress generally. A lady's maid who substituted grey silk stockings for black with her navy serge skirt and white silk blouse was soon ordered by the mistress to change them.

The rules about nursemaids wearing hats when they took the children out for walks in the park were equally strict. They were provided with black straw hats, which had to be kept firmly in position even when 'out to tea' with the children, and an outdoor uniform of grey coats and skirts. In the nursery they wore the inevitable cotton print dress with starched white apron, cap and cuffs, not unlike the uniform of a hospital nurse today.

The legendary 'nanny' always wore a white dress and a voluminous apron indoors (like cook) but of course, no cap. Outdoors, she wore a grey, dark blue or plum-coloured coat with a neat hat to match. In Victorian and Edwardian times nursery staff always wore black straw bonnets with white muslin strings when they sallied forth with the children.

Miss Helen Fox, writing from Isfield, Sussex, tells the author: 'In very smart houses during Edwardian times there was a phase when the afternoon uniform of the parlourmaid was changed from black and white to some other more artistic, but still dark, shade with toning apron, cap and cuffs. But only in very "smart" houses run by rather "advanced" ladies would this be apparent.'

However, as the twentieth century advanced still further, there was a definite move away from traditional starch and frills, although still only in the smarter, what we would call today 'trendy', families. These dolly parlourmaids began to take over the ornamental function once served by the liveried 'flunkey' in very grand households.

In a letter from Totnes, Devon, Mrs Helen Noel-Hill recalls a household where she stayed in the 'twenties, where the mistress allowed her maids large coloured ribbon bows in their hair in lieu of caps, which were 'beginning to be considered too much of a badge of servitude'.

Perhaps it was the country house where Mrs Doris Freegarde was a parlourmaid at that time. She describes her uniform, in a letter from Boscombe, Bournemouth: 'I made my own, a nice cinnamon brown dress for the afternoons with a pretty needlework short apron, not the bib type, and a big brown bow on my hair which was very fair, worn at the back of my head. I also wore brown shoes and stockings when I could afford them and white collars and cuffs made of celluloid, which could be easily slipped off and sponged.' *Brown* dresses, *celluloid* cuffs! How those stern

Victorian housekeepers would have quivered with indignation at such frivolities and folly. . . .

Curiously, although servant girls were forbidden to wear make-up or silk stockings, young men in the position of footmen were *required* to wear silk stockings on ceremonial occasions, and to powder their hair. Frederick Gorst, as footman to Lady Howard at the turn of the century, was gorgeously attired in blue plush knee breeches, white stockings, pumps with silver buckles, and a claret-coloured, swallow-tailed coat with silver buttons bearing the family crest. Of course, there was no likelihood of his being mistaken for His Lordship in this outfit, or indeed of his being taken for anything other than he was.

Aristocratic employers, while expecting humble maids to scrimp and save to buy their own uniforms, lavished money on the livery of menservants. In contrast to the little tin trunk in which a maid packed all her working and outdoor clothes, Gorst on becoming footman to the Duke of Portland (circa 1900) required: two steel cases, five feet long, three feet across and two feet high, to contain his full state and semi-state uniforms, two leather portmanteaux for his smaller liveries and personal effects and *six* hat boxes.

Footmen in the Stately Homes spent a great deal of their time changing uniforms, dressing and undressing, and of course, powdering their hair. As a young footman, Mr Gorst noticed with alarm that his hair was thinning because of the drying effect of 'violet powder' and he was in danger of becoming prematurely bald, he thought. So he experimented with hair oil as a base – in those days pomades and hair dressings were frequently home-made from such odd ingredients as hog's lard, ammonia, castor oil, scented with jessamine or rose water. After an hour on duty, the unfortunate Mr Gorst felt beads of moisture on his forehead and rushed to a mirror to find – horror! – that his 'wig' was slowly disintegrating. He had to excuse himself and go to the bathroom where he re-did his *coiffure* using the tried and tested method of violet powder and soap.

Today the seventeenth-century flunkey regalia has gradually died away, except on State occasion. But even in the 1920s footmen in service with the Earl of Londesborough in Lincolnshire wore dark blue trousers, a waistcoat with *horizontal* stripes, a stiff shirt with a wing collar and a white bow, and a tailcoat with crested silver buttons, four each side and two to fasten, link-wise.

Mr Bentinck, who was one of those footmen, writes to the author: 'Although they were given livery to wear, footmen had to buy their own dress shirts and white bows and collars. Eventually paper dress shirt fronts, cuffs and collars came in, which we bought from Thorne's of Victoria, a shop dealing in footmen's and butlers' requirements.'

The butler, king of the servants' hall, wore tails and a black tie (gentlemen always wear a *white* tie with tails) as he stood at the door to announce that dinner was served. As one guide to his duties puts it, in a manner which cannot be bettered: 'He should be simply in the plainest and best-fitting of all thoroughly plain evening dresses.'

Coachmen, who had always been among the best-dressed of servants, with their gleaming boots topped in white, brightly coloured greatcoats with silver or brass crested buttons, hats with cockades in them, slowly died out as the broughams and phaetons were replaced by Rolls-Royces and Daimlers. Their place on the box was taken by a chauffeur at the wheel, dressed, as he often is to this day, in grey with a peaked cap.

But in at least one home in the 1920s, a female domestic emerged from below stairs and challenged the dominant male of the servant class. Mrs Bishop, in a letter from Anglesey, tells me that in her parents' home one of two living-in maids did duty as *chauffeuse* and was fitted out with a grey coat, matching peaked cap and brown leather gauntlet gloves. And the chauffeur's uniform, little changed, is the only regularly seen livery of domestic service surviving into the 1970s.

9

RECRUITING THE SKIVVIES

WANTED, a cook who thoroughly understands her business, and can have an unexceptionable personal character, in a small clergyman's family 12 miles from town. Being a very comfortable situation high wages will not be given. None need apply who have not been at least a twelvemonth in their last place. Apply by letter, pre-paid stating full particulars to A.Z. post office, Loughton, Essex.

(From The Times, 1854.)

When that advertisement appeared employers could hire a parlourmaid for only £12 per annum, not even twice the cost of a year's subscription to *The Times*. For a hundred pounds a gentleman could rent elegant furnished apartments in St James's, with no extra charge for the servants. It was not at all unusual for servants to be thrown in with good quality property up for sale or rent.

There were hordes of servants in the market for 'situations'. Papers like *The Times* and the *Morning Post*, which were the favoured media for the recruiting of servants, had whole pages of nurses and housemaids (upper and lower), cooks, housekeepers, nurses, ladies' maids, parlourmaids, kitchen maids, general servants, butlers, footmen, coachmen and grooms – all wanting places. Cooks came in almost bewildering variety, describing themselves as *professed, though plain* or simply *plain, very good* plain, *thorough good* plain, or just *good*.

Choosing someone who would provide just the sort of fare you wanted must have been a daunting task, requiring calm nerves, exceptional judgement and no small degree of insight. But a lady in Beckenham engaging a cook in 1896 knew just how to go about it. (This letter was contributed by Mrs Alice M. Coleman of Raynes Park.)

'Fernside',
Albermarle Road,
Beckenham.

To Alice Arthur

I hear from Mrs Hunt that you are wishing for a situation as Cook in Beckenham and shall be glad to hear full particulars from you. Can you make good clear and thick soups, fry and serve fish in other ways also? Can you make good entrées, puff paste, creams and jellies. Roast *before* the fire and serve and dress all kinds of poultry? Are you an early riser? I am needing a good cook to go with us to Folkestone on 28th July and afterwards for Beckenham permanently. Wages £25. All found 5 in family 4 servants (cook, parlourmaid, housemaid, Valet and companion house-keeper).

MRS BRAND

Personal character required.

Servants applying for positions had on occasion to do more than prove their ability to tackle the tasks the situation required. In the following letter, written between 1867 and 1873, the Reverend Donald M. Owen advised a prospective employee, George Inch, that he would have to reduce the size of his family if he were to take up a post with him.

Marks Tey
July 2

Inch –

I can offer you Board in my House and 10s a week to your wife until I can find a suitable cottage for her here –
Then –
A Cottage furnished and Garden – rent free – Twelve Shillings a week wages – Dinner in the Kitchen every day for yourself – Livery & Stable Clothes provided –
Mrs Owen wd make some arrangement with your Wife abt Washing – I shd require you to take charge of my Horse & Carriage – And to look after Pigs & to keep my Garden in Order. This would not be light work –
My Man now gets 13s a week and some Beer – And nothing else – I cannot part with him for two or three weeks yet – so if you thought the place would suit you – I shd like to hear at once and would then fix a time for you to bring up the Horse from Exeter or Taunton
Of course you wd have to reduce your number of Children before your Wife moved

Yours faithfully
Donald M. Owen

The main source of supply of servants throughout the eighteenth and nineteenth centuries was the country, as yet unspoiled by the coming of motor transport and the intrusion of urban life. In the country men and women still used the market place as an employment exchange. Public hirings of servants called 'Mop Fairs', or simply 'The Mop', were held once or twice a year. They were servants' carnivals, ending up with drinking and dancing. Samuel Curwen, an American, attended a hiring fair at Waltham Abbey in 1782 and noted: 'Females of the domestic kind are distinguished by their aprons, viz. cooks in coloured, nursery maids in white linen and chamber and waiting maids in lawn or cambric'. The custom continued throughout the nineteenth century and survived into the twentieth in some rural areas.

An article in *Every Boy's Annual* 1871 explained why the hiring fairs continued to thrive: 'The servants must have a holiday and until a fresh scheme is adopted, they will remain true to the annual statutes. It is for want of a day's amusement that the various Servants' Registration Societies have failed. They cannot go to the seaside, to Scotland, or even take an excursion ticket; so they take and enjoy the only real holiday they have.' The speaker, Mr Elton, adds that he himself never misses 'The Mop': 'I go and see all the shows, and the Mollies and Johnnies enjoying themselves.'

Groups of servants, dressed in their best clothes, walked to the fair, along the winding lanes, past honeysuckled cottages, touching their hats to the gentry who went past them in carriages. The market place was filled with stalls, shows and people and the public houses were full. By the side of the market house the servants stood in rows like the rank and file of an army. Shepherds in embroidered smocks carried crooks, cowherds and ploughmen in velveteens carried a bit of cowhair or whipcord to denote their calling.

The writer goes on: 'On the contrary, the servant girls had no distinguishing marks to indicate their calling; although by some inscrutable means, the masters and mistresses seemed to know who had been hired, and who were still wanting places. Dairy maids and general servants were most in demand. The noise and confusion of this Babel was very great.'

The small farms were the nurseries of hard-working virtuous lads and lasses who made excellent servants. They went to the homes of the new middle classes, who employed a larger and larger proportion of the domestic labour force to work for them in the rapidly-growing towns.

The English were changing during the nineteenth century from a pastoral people to a nation of town dwellers and by 1900 more people lived in the cities than in the rural areas. Capital and labour were drawing up their battle lines; strikes and lock-outs taught both sides to respect each other's power and to negotiate, rather than fight. But none of this touched domestic service, by far the largest employer of female labour, which continued to be both plentiful and cheap.

The traditional feudal order of the countryside was a long time dying. Even when the *Daily Mail* was 'being read on the village ale bench and under the thatch of the cottage,' the lower orders still touched their hats or pulled their forelocks on meeting the village squire, or the Master and Missus, the schoolmaster or the vicar. In the towns there was no outward show of respect from the working classes to the middle classes. 'Jack' considered himself to be as good as his master.

In the country the parson invariably occupied a high social position, and this was maintained well into the twentieth century. Miss Griffith, whose father was a rector in an East Anglian village in the 1920s, wrote to the author from Heringham, Norwich: 'I think it's no exaggeration to say that the one ambition of every girl leaving school was to come to the Rectory as between-maid. I always had a waiting list of girls wanting to come to us at fourteen for £12 a year and when a vacancy was likely there was great speculation in the village as to "who will Miss Elsie send for?" With the exception of between-maids, no maid ever left us except to be married. The tweenies stayed two to four years. If I had no opportunity then to promote them in the house I found them a place with friends, with the promise that they could come back to us if they wished as cook or house parlourmaid when there was a vacancy – this they frequently did. Several times we had sisters as cook and house parlourmaid and once all three girls were sisters.'

The daughters of workers employed on estates, the system by which English agriculture was organized, were expected to start in domestic service 'up at the Hall'. They had to have a reference from the schoolmaster or the parson. Girls in large families living in rural slums were usually packed off to London with a reference from the vicar and a warning 'not to get into trouble'. Rarely did anyone bother to explain the facts of life to them before they left.

There were no Mop Fairs in the Metropolis but there were plenty of servants' registry offices. They acquired a rather dubious reputation in the eighteenth century – when one writer described them as 'warehouses of iniquity', aiding and abetting the procurement of false references and pimping as a sideline – and they never quite lost this vague aura of sin. A watercolour of 'the only reputable office in London', painted by Thomas Rowlandson in 1802, shows a raw lad just up from the country being interviewed by an imposing and amply proportioned lady with a large feather in her bonnet, and an ageing roué examining a buxom serving wench through an eyeglass, while an obese cook looks on with undisguised interest.

This was the Great Age of Servants, when the supply was plentiful and their demands for wages and nights out were still moderate. Staff who left were easily replaced and a request to a registry office would immediately produce several well-screened applicants. Girls were often lined up for prospective employers to interview and choose.

F. W. Swanson wrote in a letter to the author: 'When she wanted a maid my mother usually went to a servants' registry office and gave her requirements and was given the names and addresses and some details of girls requiring situations. Those who seemed suitable, mother made an appointment with for an interview. The girls generally arrived with their mothers, who naturally wanted to see what the new mistress was like.

'My mother always asked for a *personal* (not a written) reference and if it proved satisfactory to both sides the girl was engaged.'

During the heyday of the famous servants' agency run by Mrs Hunt in Marylebone, in the 1890s and early 1900s servant girls newly arrived from the country slept in the attics, like disposable stock, while waiting to be placed. Fashionable ladies had their own private cubicles on the premises, where they were in the habit of interviewing as many as twenty or thirty girls before deciding on one who would do as a housemaid. On the stairs was a 'roll of honour' with the names of grand clients inscribed in gold letters, together with the details of the long periods they had kept butlers, cooks and other upper servants.

The leading London agencies of the Victorian period, the impeccable Mrs Hunt's and Masseys (the latter survives to this day in Baker Street although Hunt's was eventually closed) did much towards improving the image of the trade. Mrs Hall, of Oxford, says in a letter: 'If one wrote to Masseys or Mrs Hunt, they kept records and placed servants in a good, well-recommended situation each time they asked to move.'

114

Yet the seediness of agencies as a whole persisted and there was a well-known saying: 'When down and out start an agency for servants'. Most agencies charged a shilling in the pound commission on a year's wages agreed, and they therefore had an interest in maintaining as high a turnover as possible. Each replacement meant another fee. In the 1920s agencies were still being accused of sharp practices, just as they were two hundred years previously.

A report from the chief officer of the Middlesex Public Health Control Department in 1921 referred to 'glaring instances of fraudulent advertising'. Agents were raking in fat profits by suggesting in advertisements that they could supply female Admirable Crichtons, when all they had in fact were work-shy sluts with no experience of domestic service and no desire to learn. An agent in Teddington, with several pre-war convictions for offences under the by-laws, was found to be 'defrauding the public on a wholesale scale' with bogus advertisements for servants supposed to be seeking situations, and householders – in most cases 'retired bachelor colonel' or 'young lady about to marry' – supposed to be requiring them. After a 'lengthy and difficult investigation', the agent was brought before Middlesex justices of the peace and fined £35, plus twenty-five guineas costs, and his name was struck off the Middlesex register of servants' agencies.

Under an Act of 1907 local authorities were empowered to keep a register of these agencies, but few did so, although the London County Council was one authority that kept a register and issued licences, renewed every year.

A committee of ladies set up after the 1914–18 war to advise the Minister of Reconstruction, Sir Auckland Geddes, on how best to deal with the 'domestic service problem' found at times a want of frankness on the part of registry offices about the situations to which they sent their clients. Because a separate fee was charged for each engagement, frankness was not in their own interests. Contracts between employers and servants were usually verbal, not written, and that meant that when disputes arose over hours, pay and working conditions each side had a different notion of the terms they had agreed.

Another potent source of friction was the time-honoured system of giving 'characters'. A servant was not a slave and was free to give notice and leave. But in practice, the servant was entirely dependent on the mistress for a reference, and without a satisfactory reference, stood no chance of getting another job in private service.

But a master or mistress was *not bound* to give a servant a character at all. If a character *was* given it had to be a true one, but the 'good housekeeping' books of the day never tired of warning employers that if the reference was not a good one, care should be taken with the wording, because it could be actionable. A master giving a false character of a servant in writing, knowing it to be false, and the servant unfit for a situation from drunkenness, dishonesty or some other character defect, faced a penalty of £20 and ten shillings costs. Kind hearts were not encouraged!

> Lorna - Lorna
> Bella. Vista
> Furzeham —
> Brixham —
> 14th.5.15
>
> Ethel Philips has been a servant in my employment for 5 & ½ years and during that time I have always found her a most truthful, honest & obliging girl — Clean in her habits & very hardworking — I can thoroughly recommend her as a good servant where ever she may be employed —
>
> G. Matraves

Conversely, if the employer stated that a servant, who in fact had done nothing wrong, was untrustworthy or lazy this was also actionable, provided the servant could *prove that his employer had acted with express malice*. This, of course, was no easy thing to do.

A master was under no legal obligation to prove or substantiate the truth of the character he gave and it was, in law, a privileged communication unless given maliciously. The servant would have to make out a very strong case before the question of malice was allowed to go to a jury. So if answers to inquiries about a servant were unfavourable, or even false, the servant had no right of action unless he could *prove* malice. The fact that these things might have been said in front of several people would make no difference. It was a confidential declaration in the eyes of the law.

Information about a servant obtained at second-hand could also be privileged, and a master answering inquiries about the character of a servant was entitled to say what he had been told by others if he believed it to be true. If he had given a servant a good character he could always change it in the light of later information.

Assuming that a servant, surmounting all these legal obstacles, persisted in an action against a former employer he still had to prove that the words used were actionable in themselves – that they imputed some criminal offence, contagious disease, dishonesty, immorality or something affecting him in his capacity as a servant (such as accusing a gamekeeper of killing foxes). Or he must have suffered some special damage, actual definite injury as a result of the slanderous statements. The latter was, of course, the harder to prove.

All in all, the English law hardly encouraged servants to bring actions against their employers over questions of character. But the law and the servant in so far as it was in the employers' interest, was strict and to the point: if anyone 'falsely personated' a master or his wife, housekeeper, steward or servant and gave a counterfeit character to someone seeking a situation they were liable to a fine of £20. And a similar penalty was imposed on servants for making false statements when seeking employment, or making use of a forged reference, or altering a date, erasing any word or pretending that they had never been in service on any previous occasion. This was an effective deterrent because to many a servant girl £20 represented as much as two years' wages.

A Government committee of inquiry into the recruiting of women into domestic service reported in 1923: 'Our attention has constantly been drawn to the extent to which a maid's future is at the mercy of an unjust or spiteful employer who by witholding a reference, or giving an unfair or prejudiced account of her, may easily render her chances of obtaining desirable employment very small . . . many witnesses stated that it was the fear of having short or bad references which often induced maids to remain in situations where they did not receive good treatment. Unless an employer has sufficiently definite grounds for dissatisfaction to be prepared to state them in writing, and to tell the maid at least what their general nature is, she should give a formal reference only and refrain from criticism or comment unless pressed for further detail.'

The committee was not prepared to recommend the introduction of an official system of discharge books 'such as is in vogue in some Continental countries'. There was a horror among all employers of domestic servants, from stately homes down to semi-detached suburban villas, of officialdom creeping in by the back stairs, as it were.

The State-run employment exchanges only began to act as agencies for domestic servants in private houses after the beginning of the 1914–18 war, amidst assurances from the Board of Trade that this was to be only a temporary wartime measure. It was not a success. Not only did they have the private servants' agency lobby to contend with, but they were up against innate English conservatism. Employers and servants alike were of the opinion that labour exchanges, as they were called, associated in the public mind with the *iniquitous* 'dole' and long queues of unemployed after the war, would not produce either the better class of servants or the better class of 'situations'. In 1918, after the exchanges had been handling domestic service for more than three years, the average placings per exchange were only one-and-a-half per month, yet the total numbers 'in service' at the time were around 1,200,000. The exchanges did, however, find jobs for large numbers of charwomen and 'dailies': they accounted for more than a quarter of the total vacancies for women filled in the five weeks ending 13 April 1917.

The privately run servants' registry was, and remained until domestic service itself became almost extinct, one of the main agencies for recruiting. One of the author's correspondents remembers being taken by her mother to a servants' agency in 1920, at the age of fourteen. The following conversation took place:'

Agent: Can she work hard?
Mother: She won't for me, but she might for a stranger.
Agent: Is she strong?
Mother: Seems to be.
Agent: Presumably honest and clean: Well, here's an address of a lady who wants someone for housework to live in, 5s. a week. Hard place but it's all I've got for an inexperienced girl. Go at 4 p.m. today.

118

The lady was the wife of a chemist. She asked the mother how many children she had, what the father did for a living and how much schooling the girl had had. The child was accepted for a post as maid-of-all-work in the eight-roomed, three-storey house, to start in three days' time.

She writes: 'I tolerated it, knowing I could have done something better than that. But at that time there was nothing else for the likes of me. One must stay in a job in order to get a "reference", or go begging.'

Mrs Surguy, of Aylesbury, remembers being taken to a house in Evelyn Gardens, Kensington when she was fourteen, by the Metropolitan Association for Befriending Young Servants (MABYS). The vacancy was for a tweeny. The lady of the house, having carefully inspected her from head to toe, raised her lorgnette and commented: 'She doesn't look very strong', to which the matron replied: 'No, but she's very willing.'

In London MABYS looked after orphan girls who were being 'put out to service.' A minimum wage of £5 *a year* was insisted upon (simple-minded girls were all too easily cheated by unscrupulous employers) and time off on Sundays. Records were kept and the girls out at service regularly visited. There was a hostel in Oakley Street, Chelsea, for girls out of work or between jobs, a sick fund and registry offices all over London. Other philanthropic societies with an interest in placing young girls in service were the Girls' Friendly Society, the Church Army and the Salvation Army, founded by 'General' Booth to save souls and bring practical help to the homeless and hungry, the drunkard, the criminal and the harlot.

Violet Firth, who wrote a book in 1925 on *The Psychology of the Servant Problem*, claimed that orphanages and workhouses had played a considerable part in lowering the standard of servants' conditions in England. They used to train the majority of girls in their care for service.

Miss Firth wrote: 'The placing of these girls in situations and the driving of bargains concerning their wages and conditions was done by people who were themselves of the employer caste. If a girl was discontented with the conditions and threw up her post she had no home to go to, no relations to tide her over a spell of unemployment and so enable her to hold out for better terms; she had to go back to the institution from which she came and she received scant mercy. The standard of conditions was thus forced down by what amounted to a supply of forced labour.'

Little or nothing has been written by the orphans themselves, children plucked from institutions to be a menial in someone else's kitchen. But Mrs Hilda Strange, in a letter to the author, tells of how she was recruited into service before the 1914–18 war, at the age of thirteen, from a children's home. Her father died and she was one of six children, too many for her mother to support, so with her sister she was put into a home in the parish of Sawtry in Hertfordshire where her mother was born.

One day she was skipping in the grounds when she was sent for by the Master and told to line up in the hall with other girls of her age. Some ladies had called to select girls for service. They stood there nervously, little girls in their drab institution uniform, as the visitors looked them up and down. One lady said: 'I'll have this girl. She looks healthy.' She was the wife of a local tradesman. Mrs Strange remembers her exact words to this day.

The parish union had long been a source of cheap labour in domestic service, but the *Journal of the Girls' Friendly Society* gave its opinion in 1880 that too many workhouse girls had an 'inherited disposition to vice'. They tended to grow up dull and heavy, knowing nothing of a life of freedom. But they had acquired the arts of deceit and at the age of thirteen or fourteen the only places available to them in service were those which had been rejected by girls who could afford to pick and choose. The sight of even modest luxuries demoralized them: they were unable to resist the temptations of a well-stocked larder, they picked up pretty objects which they weren't supposed to touch and tried on clothes they found lying about. They had scrubbed floors but didn't know how to clean carpets, they could handle heavy crockery but not crystal tumblers. All too often they were dismissed with no character or, just as bad, a poor one, and ended up back in the workhouse at seventeen, consumptive or pregnant, sometimes both.

In his annual report for 1915, the Chief Inspector of Reformatory and Industrial Schools said that as usual the 'disposals' from the girls' schools had been mostly into service, but he went on: 'It is evident, however, to even a casual visitor to the schools, that far from all the inmates are really suitable for this career, and it is pleasing to note an increasing tendency to place girls in other employment.'

'Practical training' was given to girls who were of an age to leave institutions like this by keeping them on to attend the chief officers as servants.

There were actually schools for servants run by local education authorities but many of them were closed down during the 1914–18 war and never re-opened. In 1914 there were ten such schools in England and Wales, four of them in the London area, and eighteen 'domestic economy schools', twelve of them in London. The latter were founded by the London County Council in 1894 to train girls, not necessarily to go into service, but as home-makers. In fact a high proportion did enter private domestic service.

Girls were taken into domestic service schools in London between the ages of thirteen and fifteen and trained for two years. Parents had to pay fees of thirty shillings [£1.50] a year (a considerable outlay for a working class family in those days) unless the girl was lucky enough to get a scholarship, awarded after an examination and interview.

School hours were nine to five, five days a week, and a third of the curriculum was devoted to general education, including reading, history, arithmetic and household accounts, singing, physical training and in some cases hygiene, infant care and first aid. The remaining two-thirds of the course was taken up with practical instruction in household work, including dressmaking, mending and darning.

At the end of the first year the pupil decided in which branch to specialize and went on to qualify as kitchen maid, scullery maid, housemaid, under parlourmaid or laundry maid and to get a job in a private house.

By the end of the war the numbers under training in these kitchen academies had dropped from 350 (in itself an infinitesimal number in view of the total servant army in England) to a mere 220, and one of the schools had closed altogether. This reflected a growing distaste among young girls for domestic service.

The 'domestic economy schools', to which scholarships were available on the recommendation of elementary school headmistresses, fared even worse. By 1918 seven of the twelve schools in London had been closed and the actual number of pupils was only 170. Half of the schools in other parts of the country had been closed. Most young girls were taking up jobs where the pay was higher than in domestic service and there was considerably more freedom.

But training for domestic service was still being given in certain boarding schools under the Poor Law Certified Schools Act, 1862. Girls who had no choice in the matter, being orphans or destitute, were drafted to these institutions by the Poor Law Guardians for 'special instruction'.

Little, if any, time was wasted on general education and the training concentrated on such matters as how to make beds and scrub floors and 'inculcation of good habits'. In some of the schools the girls did part of the household shopping or were sent out to work in the houses of local ladies who showed an interest in the schools. Otherwise they had little contact with the outside world and the low level of the instruction they received and the menial nature of the jobs they were trained for – mostly as laundry or scullery maids – gave them little opportunity to develop their minds or their personalities. There was, however, a keen demand for these girls when they were 'put out to service' at the end of their training.

Employers in the bigger houses with several servants often only engaged them through the recommendations of friends, or the servants of friends. Service was regarded as a good career by working class mothers for their less intelligent daughters as it seemed to offer a good home and security. Girls from Scotland, Wales, Ireland and Durham were employed in large numbers in London because they were believed to have the qualities needed for a good domestic: that is, they were strong and healthy.

The girls' main reasons for entering service were simply that it gave them a roof over their heads and at least three square meals a day. Parents would often write to relations already in service in a big house asking if they could 'place' young Fred or Jane. If Jane was fond of children she might get a post as under nursemaid, if she was tall and nice looking she might end up as a parlourmaid. If she was merely strong and willing, the kitchen was the place for her, but with a great deal of hard work and some luck she might eventually graduate to being a cook, and rule the roost below stairs.

Florence Faux, of Cosham writes: 'To get work in a house employing several servants [before the First World War] was almost impossible in the beginning unless you were known to the employers, either because you lived in the same village or alternatively were from an orphanage where girls had a little training in domestic work. This meant your character could be vouched for. Most people thought service, where food and lodging were assured, a better proposition than working in a shop or factory under sweated conditions. The dreadful thing to me was that though you had to have the best references, you could be turned out without a reference at the whim of a bad-tempered house-keeper or a neurotic mistress. Times didn't really alter until after the war, when for the first time, the ordinary folk were needed for more important work, and very many servants never did go back to it, especially menservants.'

In the days of high unemployment between the wars, mothers of school-leaving daughters in the Yorkshire coalfields would call at selected houses in the better parts of town to see if any help was needed. Mrs Mary Ramsden, of Barnsley, says in a letter: 'This happened to me as a young wife and I arranged that the girl, a miner's daughter, should come to "live in" at five shillings a week with a bedroom on the top floor. She stayed in the kitchen and took her meals there, too, alone. During the early years of my family, I enjoyed four such girls who were, without exception, kind, happy and well-mannered, usually leaving at sixteen years of age to continue domestic work in more wealthy homes.'

In extremity, of course, one could always advertise for a servant in the papers. In 1900 *Punch* quoted the following, from the *Irish Times*:

WANTED, a distressed lady, to mind and attend elderly lady and make herself useful about the house. Salary £7 to £8 a year to suitable person.

In the selection of footmen, calves often came before character. One such fighting cock described himself, none too modestly, in an advertisement in *The Times* in 1850 as 'tall, handsome, with broad shoulders and extensive calves'. He goes on to state that he prefers Belgravia, or the *north* side of the Park. Another footman offering his services specifies 'six months a year in town and if an incon-venient neighbourhood, five guineas extra salary'.

Not all applicants were so hard to suit, as these two advertise-ments from *The Times* in 1854 show:

NO SALARY REQUIRED: A widow lady, without family, the daughter of a clergyman, wishes a SITUATION as USEFUL COMPANION or HOUSE-KEEPER in a small family, or to superintend the household of a widower, for which she is of suitable age and quite competent. Good references can be offered. Address, pre-paid, H.H. post-office High Street, Kensington.

LADY'S MAID. Understands hairdressing, dressmaking and clear starch-ing. Age 30. Good character. No objection to do the dusting.

Dr William Kitchener, who used to churn out domestic service manuals with titles such as *The Housekeeper's Oracle* thought that the best way to obtain a servant was by the recommendation of a friend, or failing that, of the baker, butcher, poulterer, greengrocer or milkman. By the 1850s all kinds of other people were involved in the business of recruiting domestic servants, acting as clearing offices for replies to advertisements. These included libraries, post offices, newsagents and a curious establishment on Brixton Hill calling itself 'Miss Wilson's fancy warehouse.'

By the end of the nineteenth century the Great Age of Servants was on the wane. The smaller houses in the suburbs employing only one 'cook-general' were finding them hard to come by and the advertisements of the period began to show a certain wheedling turn of phrase, such as 'no children or washing' . . . 'easy place' . . .

The 'Domestic Situations' columns are a fascinating guide to the fluctuations of the market for servants. After the 1914–18 war servants were undoubtedly in short supply and therefore commanded the market. They found situations easy to get and easy to leave. Mrs Helen Morris, writing to the author from Swindon, remembers advertising her services as a cook in the *Morning Post* in 1924 and receiving sixty letters and ten telegrams from prospective employers.

This chapter opened with an advertisement from *The Times* of 1854, the same issue, as it happens, in which the famous war correspondent William Russell reported on the Charge of the Light Brigade from the Crimea. Here to end it is one from the General Strike edition of the same newspaper in 1926 which shows how the times had changed:

£52 – General wanted for small flat in S.W. district; two in family, one often away; daily outings; all labour saving devices.

10

WAGES AND 'PERKS'

In 1858 a famous correspondence was launched in *The Times* over whether a young gentleman could afford to marry on £300 a year. Among the many readers who wrote in, giving details of their budgets, was a young married gentleman doing quite nicely on £300 a year, who among his various expenditures noted: £12 6s. on the *combined* wages of a maidservant and a nursery maid, £25 on rent, £3 12s. in taxes and £22 to the butcher. So the wages of two servants were little more than half his meat bill, and after all outgoings he still had £69 14s. left – enough to employ another four or five servants had he chosen to do so.

The great age of servants was approaching its peak at that time. Servants were easy to find, required hardly any time off and no holidays, and were cheap. But over the next few decades the cost of keeping servants began to rise because so many girls and boys of an age to go into service were leaving for London and other big towns.

The following extracts from the day book of John Fortnam, Oxfordshire farmer, (supplied by Mr Malings of Rhoose, Barry), suggest that wage inflation is no new thing. The first extract relates to the housekeeper, and the others to general servants:

1864: Mrs. Ralph askd me 3s. 6d. per week but I have agreed to give her 3s. a week this is what Mrs. Malings said would be right.

1867: Mary White our servant came Tuesday, April 30th. She told us she was to have had 2£ if she had stopd at the other place.

1868: Our sirvent name Sarah Ann Wooding, Helmdon, agreed to give her £3 and if a good girl would make her a present of something in the course of the year.

1870: Servant name Elizabeth Thorn to have wages £4 if good girl and stopd all the year. Feb. 16th. She received 2s. April 12th she received £1 to go to Banbury with. do Received for her mother to pay thare rent 10s.

1871: Our servant Ann Thorn. Her wages was to be £4 and I promised to give her 5s. more if she was a good girl and stopd with us until Michaelmas.

1872 Ann Thorn our servant is to have from Michaelmas 1871 to Michaelmas 1872 £5 10s. and if she stops all the year to have £6.
[N.B. John Fortnam's spelling was entirely his own!]

Wages were paid quarterly, sometimes annually, and never in advance except for occasional disbursements 'on account' in emergencies. Anything bought for the servants was deducted by the employer, who kept a careful note in his diary . . . 'one pair of stockings 1s. 2d., two print dresses at 6s. 9d. and 3s. 9½d.', and so on.

A parlourmaid in 1884, receiving three gold sovereigns for her first quarter's pay, immediately posted them home in an envelope to her mother. Arthur Inch's mother, he recalls in a letter to the author, received one golden sovereign for three months' work at her first situation in 1890 at £4 per annum, and he adds: 'She thought herself the wealthiest young lady going. She had, I expect, up till then only handled a copper or two.'

In the early years of the twentieth century, despite general advances in wages, children of thirteen or even younger were still being employed as the 'odds and ends' of domestic service – tweenies, scullery maids, boot boys and so on – for as little as 2s. 6d. [12½p] a week, or £8 or £9 a year. But the average wage for the lowest orders in domestic service in London had reached 5s. [25p] a week.

In 1893 income tax was 7d. [less than 3p] in the £ and in 1894, amidst much disgruntled murmuring from taxpayers, it went up to 8d. But anyone earning less than £160 per annum was exempt, which included a large section of the lower middle classes who were nevertheless well off enough to employ a servant.

An assistant master at an elementary school earning less than £200 a year employed a living-in maid from the time he married in 1895 until the First World War. He paid the maid £10 a year up to 1900 and then £12 a year. His son, Mr Booth, who writes to the author from Bournemouth, says: 'We lived in the Crouch Hill district of North London on the borders of North Islington and Hornsey. Almost everyone had a maid. Both my parents had to put in much extra time in music teaching to make ends meet. The maid lived in her own little room at the top of the house. But Father never had the gas put on because he thought that would encourage the maid to read in bed! Father had to watch his expenses, so the maid went to bed with a candle.'

Moving up the social scale, a bank manager in Hertford with £600 a year, plus a free seven-bedroomed house with three-quarters of an acre for a garden, employed between 1897 and 1911 a housemaid (£12–16 p.a.) and a cook (£16–20 p.a.) with, of course, free board and lodging. He had four children and a 'knife-boy' who called every day, and who for a shilling [5p] a day not only cleaned the knives, but also the family's boots and shoes, brought in the coal for six or seven fires, chopped the wood and bathed the dog. The one-day-a-week gardener was paid 2s. 6d. [12½p], rising to 4s. 6d. [22½p], and brought his own sandwiches. And out of that £600 – a very handsome salary in the 1890s – the bank manager also employed a living-in nursemaid or governess before the children were sent off to boarding school. (Information in a letter to the author from H. C. Cosens, Sandhurst Cross.)

During the same period, as recorded by Charles Booth in *Life and Labour of the People of London*, the average wages for footmen, related to height, were as follows:

2nd footman, 5ft. 6ins. £20–22; 5ft. 10ins. to 6ft. £28–30.
1st footman, 5ft. 6ins. up to £30; 5ft. 10ins. to 6ft. £32–40.

Frederick Gorst, as a junior royal footman to the Duke of Portland during King Edward VII's reign, was paid the princely salary of £100 a year. In his book *Of Carriages and Kings*, he recollects that he was paid by a cheque which was in itself an extraordinary piece of engraving: it measured eight inches by twelve inches. The recipient tore off the lower half, which he exchanged for his wages in cash. The top half was signed as a receipt and returned to the office at Buckingham Palace. He writes: 'The cheque looked more like a diploma than legal tender.' Footmen in a mere earl's home were only required to go into the butler's pantry and sign for their wages, a customary procedure even for humble maids earning only £9 a year.

The following comparison of servants employed by a solicitor and a curate at the turn of the twentieth century is compiled from letters to the author from their descendants.

The solicitor commuting daily from Teddington to London in 1900 employed a cook at £30 a year, a house parlourmaid at £25, a tweeny at £14 a year and a boot and knife boy at 5s. [25p] a week. He could buy six shirts for £1 10s. [£1.50], champagne was £2. 8s. [£2.40] for a dozen bottles and first rate cigars 16s. [80p] *per hundred*. Cigarettes were five for a 1d., beer 2d. a pint, but tea was relatively expensive at 1s. [5p] or 1s. 6d. [7½p] a pound. A house could be well furnished for £100.

An assistant curate of the Church of England on £120 a year when he married in 1905, engaged a living-in maid at £12 a year. Later he became rector of a parish in Northants during the First World War and had to pay £15 for a maid. She was the daughter of a farm labourer who said her father's employer had been very generous at Christmas, presenting him with two pigs' ears and a pig's tail. She said they had made them into brawn as a feast for the whole family. The rent paid by some farm labourers for their cottages at that time was only 1s. 6d. [7½p] a week.

By 1910 mistresses were grumbling at having to pay a cook £26 a year – ten shillings [50p] a week. In the following year they must have been outraged even more when Mr Lloyd George, as Chancellor of the Exchequer, brought in the National Insurance Bill. The effect of this on domestic service was that mistresses and maid had to contribute 3d. a week each [rather less than 1½p] to insure the latter against illness.

Employers of servants fought the Bill tooth and nail led by Northcliffe's *Daily Mail*, calling for a 'strike' of mistresses against the tax. One defiant English lady, quoted in E. S. Turner's *What the Butler Saw*, claimed she had employed servants for seventy years and always given them the best of medical attention when they needed it, free. She declared that it 'remained to be seen' whether she would be dragged off to prison for refusing to pay the infamous tax, if it became law.

Even medical opinion was enlisted in the fight against what became irreverently known throughout the land as the 'Stick and Lick Bill', because it involved sticking stamps on little cards. Doctors were quoted in the *Daily Mail* on the dangers of licking stamps, a disgusting German habit apparently repugnant to Englishmen (although presumably they, or their servants, licked postage stamps?). The Medical Officer of Health for Onsett in Essex went so far as to say he would have no hesitation in destroying all stamped cards found in an infected house.

Petitions were got up, which were signed by employers and their servants, many no doubt under duress. One young servant girl who refused to sign such a petition recalls the vicar calling to ask her to change her mind, and when she refused, telling her she was a *very wicked girl*. 'I had plenty of black looks from the mistress and master.' (Violet Turner, of Faversham, in a letter to the author.)

And, of course, the 'Stick and Lick Bill' provided the music halls

Indoor staff and stable staff at Doxford Hall,
near Ellingham, *c.* 1890

Above left: Mary Webster, housekeepe at Erddig

Above: Maid in a cap, photograph by Julia Margaret Cameron, 1860s

Maids at Brandeston Hall, *c.* 1909

Mr F. Pink, coachman to
the Rawson family of
Haugh End, Sowerby,
from 1920 to 1925

Gamekeeper
at Erddig

Above: Nurse and baby on the beach at Southend

Left: Nurse, *c.* 1900

Below: Nursemaids and children in Kensington Gardens, 1913

Above right: Queen Victoria at home with her lady's maid, 1896

Right: Victorian lady being dressed, 1865

Preparing the evening meal
...rton House, near Petworth,
...95

...left: *The Finishing Touch*,
...ertisement for Lemco, 1901

: *Superior Education*

...: *A Black Indignity*

SUPERIOR EDUCATION.

Page Boy (to Jeames). "WHERE SHALL I PUT THIS 'ERE DISH OF AMMONDS?"
Jeames (with dignity). "I'M SURPRISED, HARTHUR, THAT AT YOUR HAGE YOU
'AVEN'T LEARNT 'OW TO PERNOUNCE THE *HAR* IN HARMONDS!"

A BLACK INDIGNITY.

...dy of the House. "OH, THOMAS! HAVE THE GOODNESS TO TAKE UP SOME COALS INTO THE NURSERY!"
...omas. "H'M, MA'AM! IF YOU ASK IT AS A FAVOUR, MA'AM, I DON'T SO MUCH OBJECT; BUT I 'OPE YOU DON'T TAKE ME FOR AN 'OUSEMAID, MA'AM!"

Above left: A maid using a house telephone, showing servants where in the house services are required. Photograph taken for The Sterling Telephone & Electric Co. L London, 1912

Above right: Parlourmaid preparing a bath before dinner, London, 1930s

Below: Another servant in the house this Christmas. Advertisement for the Western Ele Vacuum Sweeper, 1923

Another servant in the house this Christmas

Western Electric
VACUUM SWEEPER
WITH   THE   MOTOR   DRIVEN   BRUSH

Obtainable of WESTERN ELECTRIC COMPANY, LIMITED (Wholesale only).
Agents: H. S. COOKE, 24, St. Paul's Square, Birmingham, and ELECTRIC DISTRIBUTING COMPANY, 87, Bridge St, Manchester.

with an opportunity for laughs at the servants' expense. A typical scene depicted a grubby 'slavey' from the kitchen with stamps stuck all over her face and clothes. The mistress would ask: 'Whatever is the matter with you, Mary Jane?' and the reply: 'You told me to stick 'em on meself, Mum' no doubt brought the house down.

The climax of all the sound and fury against the Bill was a mass meeting at the Albert Hall in London, attended by two thousand people. Two days earlier Mr Lloyd George had invited a party of mistresses and maids to the Treasury and tried to explain to them that the simple object of the Bill was to guarantee 7s. 6d. a week [37½ p] sick benefit for twenty-six weeks and free medical attention.

In the event the Bill became law and from then on 'the stamp' became a feature of domestic service. But when state welfare was extended after the 1914–18 war to unemployment insurance and payment of benefits to the out of work – the 'dole' – it applied only to workers who were employed 'in any trade or business carried on for the purpose of gain', so employment in a private house as a servant was excluded. Despite this, a vast body of employers of servants was quite convinced that domestic labour after the war was in short supply because servants preferred to stay idle and draw the 'dole' – but of this, more in a later chapter.

After the 1914–18 war wages in domestic service began to rise more steeply, but only for those with specific skills to offer, cooks particularly. The 'slaveys' and 'skivvies', ignorant young girls from poor homes, were still employed for much the same pittances that their mothers had received in the 1890s. A young girl who left South Wales for London in 1927 for service and five shillings [25p] a week to escape the miseries of the depression in the aftermath of the General Strike says in a letter that she rose at 6 a.m. and was 'lucky if she got to bed at 11 p.m.'

Out of her five shillings she had to buy a morning and afternoon uniform, send what money she could to her family at home, dress herself and try to keep enough to take a bus ride or go to a cinema on her one half day a week.

Mrs Beatty, of Swindon, sent the author some extracts from a notebook she kept between 1911 and 1921 which give some idea of the struggle a middle class housewife had to keep servants, and the amount of book-keeping involved. At the start she paid her cook £20 per annum and a parlourmaid £14. The wages were paid monthly and entered meticulously in the book (£1 13s. 4d. for cook, £1 3s. 4d. for the parlourmaid).

In August 1912 the first entries occur for the iniquitous 'stamp' – 2s. [10p] a month, of which the servants pay half, so their monthly payment is reduced accordingly. Cook, for instance, now received £1 12s. 4d.

In July 1913 cook's wages went up by £2 a month to £22 and in the same year a new house parlourmaid was recruited at the same wage as the old one. In July 1914 a nurse was engaged at £22 a year.

From 1915 onwards a series of 'cook-generals' come and go, all earning £22 a year, and a nursery maid is taken on at £9 a year.

In 1918 Mrs Beatty engaged a fifteen-year-old named Kathleen as 'between-maid' or tweeny at £6 a year. She started in April and left in June, having been paid exactly thirty shillings [£1.50]. Annie, another £6-a-year tweeny, came in July and left the following February, despite having her wages raised to £10 per annum in November. Edith, a day-maid (not living in) was hired when Annie left, worked for one week and was 'sent away Feb. 20th'. By 1921 the wages of the cook-general had gone up to £32 per annum and the house parlourmaid to £28.

A sub-committee of the Women's Advisory Committee, which gave its attention to the domestic service 'problem' immediately after the 1914–18 war, drew up the following proposed scale of weekly wages with food:

	£	s.	d.
Housekeepers	1	2	6
Assistant housekeepers		18	6
Cooks with kitchen and scullery maids	1	2	6
Cook/housekeepers	1	5	0
Cooks with kitchen maids		19	6
Cooks with between-maid		17	6
Cooks single-handed		17	6
Cooks general		15	0
General domestic workers (unskilled)		12	0
—ditto— (skilled)		15	0
Head kitchen maid of two		15	0
Kitchen maid with scullery maid		12	6
Kitchen maid, single-handed		12	6
Kitchen maid, second		10	0
Scullery maid		7	6
Between-maid		7	6
Head housemaid		15	0

	£	s.	d.
Housemaid, second		12	6
Housemaid, under		7	6
House Parlourmaid		12	6
Head Parlourmaid	1	0	0
Second Parlourmaid		15	0
Head nurse	1	0	0
Second nurse		15	0
Under nurse		10	0
Lady's maid	1	0	0
Young ladies' maid		15	0
Head laundry maid		18	0
Second laundry maid		12	6
Laundry maid, single-handed		15	0
Head Still Room Maid		18	6
Second Still Room Maid		12	6
Still Room Maid, single-handed		15	0
Head Dairy Maid		15	0
Second Dairy Maid		10	0

This scale was drawn up in fact by three members of the sub-committee – Jessie Stephen, Alice Jarrett and Rosalind J. Whyatt – who also recommended a sliding scale from 6s. 6d. to 10s. for fourteen to eighteen-year-olds 'if absolutely unskilled', a minimum of 9d. per hour for daily domestic workers, and overtime rates for extra hours over eight a day, exclusive of mealtimes and time off.

Needless to say, these proposals were not adopted even by the sub-committee, who observed in their report: 'We make no recommendation with regard to definite rates of wages. As there is at present no fixed standard of efficiency, we regard a definite scale as unpracticable. On the whole, wages of domestic workers compare favourably with those in other occupations for women, though in a very few cases very low rates are still paid.'

So servants' wages continued to vary according to the employers' assessments of abilities and skills, and the laws of supply and demand. Despite all the difficulties experienced by middle class homes in London and the other large cities in finding suitable servants, despite the higher wages offered in the cities, families in provincial towns seemed to be able to recruit quite happily at wages they could afford to pay. In these towns the opportunities for women in occupations other than domestic service did not expand so rapidly.

Jean Hunt, of Farnham, recalls in a letter to the author that in 1922 all their neighbours in Bangor, North Wales – college professors, business people, solicitors – had one if not two maids. Even junior lecturers, if they had children, usually managed to keep a girl as a general maid at ten shillings a week. Her own parents employed a cook at £1 a week and housemaid – 'always a little girl straight from school, who was "trained" by my mother' – for about ten shillings [50p] increasing as she got older.

'In 1929 in Middlesbrough it was still possible to hire a resident cook-general to do all the housework and washing and most of the cooking for ten shillings a week, uniform and "stamp" provided.' (Letter from a former employer.)

Another of the author's correspondents sent the following indication of how 'nanny's' financial position improved over the years:

1870: £20 p.a. for a head nurse with four nursery maids to help her look after nine children, including two sets of twins.
1914: 'Nanny' looking after three children, £35 p.a.
1939: £100 a year for head nurse.

And Marjorie Young, who left her native Northumberland on 1 April 1925, complete with tin trunk and uniform, to go into service as a kitchen maid at Seaford, Sussex, sent the author this example of how the wages 'ladder' was climbed: 'After eighteen months in the kitchen at £20 a year, I took a job as third housemaid of three in Surrey at £26. After six months I was promoted to second (£30). After 4½ years, I went as second of four in a viscount's home (£42) and left to be a head housemaid for another viscount (£52). In 1935 a lady offered me a post as head housemaid in Hampshire at £60 a year.'

In the 1920s, these were the wages paid to the staff on the country estate of a shipping magnate in Cheshire: ten household servants were led by the housekeeper (£60 p.a.), cook (£50) and parlourmaid (£45). The tweeny got £15–20 a year. Outdoors, the head gardener earned £3 a week with a free cottage, coals, vegetables and light. He controlled seven or eight under-gardeners whose wages varied from £2 a week down to 8s. or 10s. [50p] a week for the garden boy. The chauffeur employed to drive and look after two Rolls-Royces and an Austin had £2. 10s. [£2.50] a week, with a free house, coals, vegetables and light (details from a letter).

As a butler at Nidd Hall in Yorkshire between 1923 and 1934,

John Henry Inch earned £120 a year, plus a free house, with electricity provided from the estate generator, and free wood for his fires. There were four menservants in the pantry, three kitchen staff, four housemaids and a housekeeper. His son, Arthur, started in service as a boy in 1931 at £26 p.a. and when he left to join the Royal Air Force shortly after the outbreak of the Second World War he had risen to under-butler, earning £80 a year.

Employers always undertook to provide food and lodging as well as paying a wage, but servants usually had to pay for laundry and there were 'stoppages' if they broke anything. And there was also a rather antique and complex arrangement of allowances, in addition to wages, and other 'perks' for servants.

Men in the service of the Earl of Londesborough in 1928 were still paid 3d. a day 'beer money', a quaint survival of the days when servants drank beer instead of tea. Even housemaids at Hatfield House, the seat of the Salisburys, were paid two shillings [10p] a week beer money in the early part of the twentieth century. They also had two shillings a week 'washing money', the reason for which is obscure since they did their own washing as well as that of the family.

'Board wages', sums in place of the meals normally provided, were paid by the larger households while the master and his family were away travelling or at another residence. The practice was a survival from the eighteenth century when it was criticized on the grounds that it put money in servants' pockets to 'squander in gaming, drunkenness and extravagance.'

Certainly, an astute servant could pocket his 'board wages' and eat free in the servants' hall of neighbouring houses where he had friends, for whom he would perform a similar charity when *their* families were away. In any case, the practice survived for as long as domestic service itself. In the 1930s Arthur Inch, as a butler in a large household received eighteen shillings a week board wages when the family was away. Girls would receive sixteen shillings or less, the assumption being that they could survive on a lighter diet.

Families often went abroad or shut up their houses for a period, and apart from those who were left behind on board wages, veritable armies of nurses and nursery maids, governesses, ladies' maids, valets, chauffeurs and sometimes footmen and grooms accompanied them on visits or holidays lasting for weeks or even months. Visiting servants were entertained as guests below stairs.

Another useful addition to a servant's wages, as with the staffs of hotels and restaurants, came in the form of tips from guests. 'I used to look forward to a visitor coming as they usually left a tip, perhaps 2s. 6d. [12½p], and I would send it home when I got out, as my parents were very poor.' (Former tweeny, 1918, in a letter to the author.)

But collection of tips in Victorian private houses was nothing like as well organized as the system of 'vails', a survival of an ancient form of largess, which operated in eighteenth-century households. In some cases the value of a month's 'vails' might be as much as the wages paid and, when a guest was leaving, the servants ranged themselves in two files flanking the door, each expecting a 'tip' as the guest walked past. The amount expected depended partly on the social status of the family who were the hosts and partly on the rank of the servant himself. In some great houses there was what amounted to a fixed schedule of service charges; so much for having tea, so much for breakfast in one's room and so on. As one outraged German nobleman, Baron de Pollnitz, remarked in 1738 after a visit to a stately English home: '. . . if a Duke gives me Dinner four Times a Week, his Footmen would pocket as much of my Money as would serve my Expenses at the Tavern for a Week. . . .'

The system of vails was largely stamped out in English households by the end of the eighteenth century, but something very like it reappeared when King Edward VII, a hundred years later, made 'weekends out of town' fashionable.

'Madge' [Mrs Humphry], writing in *Every Woman's Encyclopaedia* in 1910, the final year of the Edwardian era, remarks on the free and easy manners at these gatherings compared with the Victorian period, and goes on: 'In addition to valets and lady's maids, the upper class hostess is now expected to house chauffeurs as well. Taking everything into consideration, a hostess is rather more like the manageress of a hotel than the owner of a private house during the visiting season. . . . The question of tipping servants arises at the end of a visit.

'Like all things, tips have increased in amount during the last fifteen years. Menservants expect far more than in former years. There is now the host's chauffeur, too, to reckon with, and his demands are not small. An extraordinary custom is permitted at a few country houses. On the day when a guest terminates a visit the menservants are allowed to throw themselves in his or her way, and they have to be tipped. On the other hand, it is the rule in some country houses to forbid tips. In such cases the hostess makes some special arrangement with her servants. Otherwise they would consider themselves ill-used, for tips amount to large sums in houses where constant relays of guests are entertained.

'The amount given as a tip depends on circumstances and particularly on the position and social standing of the visitor. The following remarks apply to guests in the same set as their host, who is supposed to be a man of the wealthy upper classes. The butler will expect a sovereign for a few days' visit. If there have been many motor car rides, the chauffeur will expect from half a sovereign upwards. If he only meets the guest at the station and drives him back to it, five shillings [25p] or three half crowns [37½p] will do. This, too, will meet the case of a woman visitor. For a week-end visit she will give five shillings to the maid who looks after her room, half a crown [12½p] to the footman or parlourmaid who carries down her luggage when she is leaving, and a similar amount to the coachman who drives her to the station.

'A chauffeur will expect more. If her luggage is being sent on in another vehicle, she will find the driver of it waiting to be remembered. At the conclusion of a ten days' visit to a house where there is shooting the money spent on tips sometimes amounts to £5.'

Servants had other 'perks', too. Butlers were traditionally permitted to sell candle ends and old bottles. Cook was allowed to sell kitchen 'stuff' such as dripping, bones and chunks of fat.

But Mary Jewry, the author of *Warne's Model Cookery* had her own ideas about this, too: 'Do not allow dripping or bones to become a perquisite of the cook. Dripping is most useful in a moderate family.' The same author goes on to warn: 'Take care that the butcher always brings a ticket of weight with the meat; and have those weight tickets brought to you weekly in order that you may compare them with the entries in your book. All meat brought into the house should be weighed to see if the ticket is correct, and for this purpose a pair of scales should be kept in the kitchen. Groceries, &c., should also be tested as to weight on receipt of them. . . .'

Dishonest cooks, butlers and housekeepers had ample opportunity for cheating their employers and lining their own pockets. They dealt with the tradesmen, many of whom sought their favour with little 'extras', Christmas boxes and by outright bribery. It can be assumed, however, that the majority of these servants were scrupulously honest, and if they were not, they were soon found out and sent packing without a 'character'.

Throughout the hundred years covered by this book, scandalously low wages, never more than a few shillings a week, were paid to children starting in service. They were the raw material of domestic service, but they were no worse off than beginners in other fields – Lancashire mill girls, apprentices in industry, articled clerks who sometimes had to work for a year with no money at all, and those office boys of the 1890s who got only four or six shillings a week and had to keep themselves.

For the clever, presentable boy or girl domestic service gave a chance to 'better themselves'. A middle-ranking servant between the two world wars who had £30 to £50 a year pocket money, and food and accommodation provided free, was materially better off than the shop girl or factory hand who affected to despise her. However, only those who were able to get to the top of their trade managed to reach £100 a year, or £2 a week, by the time the Second World War intervened. After the war no amount of wages could coax them back into service.

11
HIGH JINKS
BELOW STAIRS

In view of their long hours and minimal time off, it is surprising that servants were able to laugh and sing at their work, but they did. Indeed, this is one of the outstanding features of the many letters written to the author by former servants and the people who employed them – the amount of fun they managed to have below stairs. Of course, there were harsh, even tyrannical, employers, and there were servants who were desperately oppressed and unhappy in service, but through it all one can detect a strong vein of humour, the ability to laugh at the grimness of life and to extract a few crumbs of happiness. It was worse, of course, for the girl who was alone, as the one servant employed in a lower middle class home, but even there life was not one of unrelieved gloom.

A letter to the author recalling childhood visits to the hop gardens of Kent at the turn of the twentieth century during the holidays, says of the maid-of-all-work who went with the family: 'It must have been a welcome escape from the house. There was much talking and singing and visits to the oast house to roast potatoes. The men workers would tease the girl, particularly on the last day when you had to avoid being 'put in the bin'. The farmer would give the young people damson wine and they would get rather wild. Our maid would arrive home with a red face, and her hat on crooked, and mother would look vexed.

'Anyway, she had a good time and I suppose it was the only holiday she had. When you think of her unremitting toil in the house, you wonder how anyone could have gone about those endless chores *singing*.'

Jean Hunt writes to the author from Farnham of the period between the wars: 'I can well remember standing at the top of the "kitchen stairs" in my grandmother's Welsh home and listening to gales of laughter coming from down in the kitchen, which had a large light window, the house being built on a hill. Although they did not go out in the evenings and didn't have a radio or television, they seemed to enjoy themselves. Nobody imagined they would want to go out – what for? If they wanted fresh air, they could walk round the garden, and often did, often with their knitting as they strolled about (but not in the front garden!). They were always happy and smiley: I can never remember a grumpy one, except one – called Adelaide – and she had adenoids, which I thought strange as it matched her name. She stands out as a grumpy exception. To us now it seems a claustrophobic existence. But to that age group it seemed natural. They went home on Mother's Day with cakes from my grandmother and usually jam and other things, but they only stayed at home if a parent were ill and my grandmother gave them leave off.'

Eileen Morris, who went into service in 1910 from a village school in Sussex, says in a letter: 'The whole family took a great interest in singing and we used to go into the drawing room to practise. My sister, who worked in the same house, won a medal at a singing festival in Tunbridge Wells. I remember the lady often coming into the kitchen at nine o'clock at night and saying: "That child should be in bed, late hours are not good for her." I was the same age as one of her own children. It was a very happy home.'

Another former tweeny in 1934 remembers in a letter to the author her monthly visit, twelve miles by bus, to her parents' home in the country: 'It was always a happy time, to be amongst my own folks again with the boyfriend there as well. On the Sunday there was always a big spread put on for tea. After tea we put on a musical entertainment which consisted of the mandolin played by Dad and the violin played by a friend, and the piano accompaniment by "Tweeny" . . . with songs by all the company. This little, gay party lasted me until next month, and sometimes out of my meagre pay, I'd be able to afford a new piece of music.'

Mass tastes in entertainment were simple and undemanding, yet many of the songs whistled by butchers' boys, scullery maids and tweenies in the 1890s are still remembered. They brightened the drabness of the long working day. These songs originated in the music halls where the cheapest seat in the house was a six-penny [2½p] place in the gallery, or 'Gods'. Even that was too much for most young girls in service. They had to find a young man to treat them to a night out.

Even before gramophone records arrived to commercialize the

process, popular songs spread quickly across the land. Barrel
organs played them in the streets and the humble skivvy scrubbing the area steps, washing pots and pans in the scullery or
cleaning boots in the 'boot hole' quickly picked up the tunes of
ditties like 'Where Did You Get That Hat?' (1888), 'Ta-Ra-Ra
Boom De-Ay' (1898) or 'Only A Bird In a Gilded Cage' (1899).
Marie Lloyd, the daughter of a waiter, specialized in 'saucy' Cock-
ney songs like 'Then You Wink the Other Eye' and 'A Little of
What You Fancy Does You Good', songs which made her famous
in the 1890s.

And, of course, the new craze of bicycling and 'bifurcated
garments' for ladies, which Mrs Bloomer had popularized in
America inspired a whole crop of music hall lyrics such as:

> My eye! Here's a lady bicyclist!
> Look at her! Look at her! Look at her!
> Hi! Hi! Hi!
> She's put her petticoats up the spout,
> And now she has to go without;
> And thinks they won't be missed . . .

Marie Lloyd warbled: 'Well what do you see? Eh, boys?', while
Katie Lawrence, in bloomers, first sang in 1892:

> Daisy, Daisy, give me your answer true.
> I'm half crazy, all for the love of you!
> It won't be a stylish marriage.
> I can't afford a carriage,
> But you'll look sweet
> Upon the seat
> Of a bicycle built for two!

In its early days, cycling attracted young ladies as well as shop
girls and servants. Millicent Wardroper, who was born in January
1879, the daughter of a solicitor, recalls in a letter to the author
that by the 1890s, 'Cycling had become the rage. Pneumatic tyres
had replaced the cushion ones, but as yet, no free-wheel, so one
had to "coast" downhill by putting up the feet on to a bar under
the handlebars. I remember once, it was ironical, we had left our
home at Putney for Brighton at 7.30 in the morning, a wet, dismal
day with a strong headwind. At Tooting I'd skidded on a big stone
(the roads weren't macadamized then), fallen off my bike and
broken my brake. We reached the long last hill down to Preston
Park at 6 p.m. – "Coasting" – where two policemen stood with a

stop watch and outstretched arms. We (my brother and I) were summoned for "scorching" – after a 10½ hours run . . .'

But the upper middle classes abandoned cycling when it became popular among the 'lower middles' and the working classes. Few servant girls could afford to *buy* a bicycle but they could hire them on their afternoons out, and they could be seen in droves coasting perilously down steep hills in Surrey and Kent with their long skirts billowing in the slipstream. By the late 1890s the new Coventry bikes with light frames and acetylene lamps were everywhere on the roads, and those who aspired to cut a little more dash went in for tweed caps and knickers and a low, crouching position over drop handlebars.

The bicycle brought a freedom to the working classes they'd never had before: the ability to roam at will about the land. The servant could escape with friends for an hour or two from the endless round of drudgery and go swishing through quiet country lanes, over the hills and away.

Unfortunately, class distinctions were applied in sports and pastimes, as in every other sphere of English life. Tennis, for example, was a middle class game. Servants did not play tennis, unless they managed to snatch an illicit hour or two on the court, in a cap and apron, while the 'family' were out.

As a parlourmaid in 1926, Miss Gerdgoens joined a church club for girls which during the summer booked a tennis court in the local recreation ground. She writes: 'Oh, the ridicule I had to go through each time I set out with my racquet and shoes because I was "aping my betters." How could a *maid* play tennis? Why we were seen as a different species I'll never know.'

Servants had, after all, little enough chance to meet people outside their own little world below stairs. In country houses it could be a mile or more from the front door to the lodge gates and the only time the staff got out was when they went to church on Sundays.

During the Victorian period, an annual visit to the Mop Fair was the most such servitors could expect in the way of entertainment, or on rare occasions (until the practice was discontinued in 1866) a public hanging. The latter was a favoured spectator sport of the lower classes. When a pot-boy called John Lawrence was hanged at Horsham in 1844 for the murder of the Chief Constable of Brighton, crowds flocked to the town from far and wide. A local publican was heard to remark that in view of all the extra trade he hoped 'a man might be hung in Horsham every day'.

By the end of the nineteenth century the range of diversions in the capital was more varied. There was George Robey, the 'Prime Minister of Mirth,' at the Pavilion, Lottie Collins at the New Cross Empire and Kate Tyndal reciting Rudyard Kipling's new war poem 'The Absent-Minded Beggar' at the Tivoli nightly, and at the Oxford an hour later, and countless other expositions, exhibitions and even *moving pictures*.

London had something to suit the leisure tastes of all classes and conditions of the population. A couple of off-duty footmen could have a few beers and a lobster dinner in Soho, go on to the Criterion to see 'The Flying Pretzels' – German acrobats on bicycles – and round off the evening with a visit to the Earl's Court Exposition to sample the lager beer on tap at the American stand.

An under-housemaid in her Sunday 'best' could spend a few of her hard-earned pence in a teashop, for the simple pleasure of being waited upon herself for a change, and go on to see the moving pictures on the American Biograph at the Palace, or the Royal Biorama at Olympia. In 1899 the Grand National was 'bio-scoped' and shown at the Palace the same evening by special arrangement with the London and North Western Railway Company, who provided a fast train from Liverpool with a special dark-room on board.

Two humble tweenies on their afternoon out might take a walk 'up West' to look at the swells, or stroll in one of the great London parks making eyes at the soldiers in their pillbox hats, tight trousers and red tunics. There was always an affinity between those in domestic service and the 'other ranks' of the Army. They, too, were often looked down upon by the public at large, as Kipling pointed out:

> It's Tommy this and Tommy that, an' 'Chuck 'im
> out, the brute!'
> But it's 'Saviour of 'is country' when the guns
> begin to shoot.

Yes, servants in London at any rate could always find somewhere to go when they were allowed out. And there were, too, some organized jollifications for domestic servants. As we saw in Chapter 2, soon after the accession of King Edward VII to the throne in 1901, Queen Alexandra decided that ten thousand London housemaids should be invited to a series of 'Queen's Teas'. The task of organizing them was given to the Bishop of London and after many drawing room conferences by committees of ladies, horse buses were hired and hundreds of girls in caps and aprons paraded in some thirty districts. They were served with 'Strawberry teas' and buns by their mistresses. They sallied forth to Hampstead Heath and other suitable spaces on 'nature rambles', they had sing-songs and visited Regent's Park Zoo, under a banner reading: 'God Bless Our Gracious Queen, the Giver of Our Feast.' Some of the festivities were marred by an English summer downpour, but the whole exercise in what would now be called public relations, was voted a huge success and the servants were returned to their places in plenty of time to get on with serving late dinner.

Employers sometimes held a servants' ball, which normally started in the early evening and ended promptly at ten. Maidservants were allowed to invite male relatives or 'serious and regular followers'. Substantial supplies of cake, oranges and nuts, and a moderate amount of beer and wine, were laid on. A correspondent who was seventh housemaid at Hatfield House in the early 1900s says in a letter, 'We had a very nice servants' ball about February, so we all had to learn to dance before that by having dancing lessons once a week from about September.' In London in the 1920s an annual ball for servants was held at the Albert Hall.

All in all, employers liked to keep a watchful and paternal eye on the leisure activities of their domestic staffs, particularly the female members. Lily Graham writes of her days as a very young tweeny in a big London house in 1906: 'I remember having to stay alone downstairs while the other staff skipped out in the evening, I was supposed to put the light off and let them in when they returned.

'One evening the mistress called all the servants in turn. Finally when I answered she said: "And who are you?" She had never seen me or even known my name. She instructed me to go past the drawing room at ten every night, so that she could hear me going to bed then, which was the official bedtime. Of course, the other servants were annoyed about having been found out, and they made me go up and then sneak down again whenever it suited them.'

Some employers laid great stress on the importance of fresh air and exercise. The Duchess of Portland insisted on her footmen exercising so that they wouldn't get too fat from all the beer they drank, and presented each of them with a bicycle and a set of golf clubs. She also engaged a diminutive Japanese judo expert, who used to throw a six-foot flunkey around the gymnasium with the greatest of ease!

A country vicar's wife, writing of the year 1910, tells the author that she always gave her servants time off every afternoon to go for a compulsory walk, but most servant girls, in the intervals between chores, were prone to spend their time reading escapist literature, penny novelettes with titles like *Kitty, Lil and Another* and *Bettie's Mistake*. The birth of a popular mass-circulation press in England towards the end of the nineteenth century also brought forth reams of pulp magazines aimed at the half-educated working girl. 'Most of their "off-hours" in the 1920s were spent reading *Eve's Own* or *Red Letter* to which my mother's only objection was that they passed these secretly on to a child – to wit, myself!' (Miss Salzedo, Hampstead.)

A vicar's daughter, in a letter, remembers a maid in her father's house in the 1920s: 'During her hour off in the afternoon, I remember her sitting on a hard chair in the kitchen reading a magazine called *Red Letter*. Her pay was ten shillings a week. Later this was increased and I remember my mother being very annoyed because Mary spent it all on *silk* underwear. Yet Mary was happy and we looked upon her as a friend. I particularly used her in many ways, such as smuggling out my love letters to unwelcome admirers (unwelcome by my father, as he was very severe with his daughters).'

After the 1914–18 war the numbers of diversions and amusements open to servants, like the rest of the working population, increased. Some servants' halls had a wind-up gramophone and a few 'Rag Time' records. The maids could have an impromptu dance with the footmen, or among themselves.

Mrs O'Donnell writes of her days as a tweeny in a manor house in 1924: 'The kitchen was our sitting room, very big with two wooden tables and three wooden chairs (no cushions).

'We were all pop music mad for it was the early days of the Charleston. My friend and I mastered it by hanging on to the backs of our chairs, until in would come the mistress saying: "Whatever is all this dreadful noise?". . .'

Mrs Marjorie Vanderson, of Gosforth, writes of the time she worked as a housemaid (1937–40): 'It was a village where we lived and if you wanted to go to the local dances it was allowed, but not until we had finished our duties, so we were always late. Some of our friends who worked in other houses were not allowed to go to any of the dances, and thought us very lucky. We had a nice sitting room for our leisure (three servants: cook, parlourmaid and housemaid). There was a radio in the drawing room and we had a loudspeaker in our room. The only snag was if "they" didn't like the programme, it was turned off. . . .'

Radio, starting in the 1920s at Savoy Hill, brought a new influence into the home, but it was the cinema more than any other entertainment that added a new dimension to the life of a girl in service. It opened up tempting horizons, tempting but forbidden to the domestic servant class. Electric Palaces, Gems, Coronations and Astorias opened up in every town. Unlike the music hall, they did not have the approval of the employers, who were quick to recognize the subversive qualities of the new medium. Attempts were made by the church to classify 'going to the flicks' as a sin, but to no avail, this avenue of escape for the slavies and skivvies was not to be denied. In the darkness of the cinema, where their shabby hand-me-down clothes and work-roughened hands went unnoticed, they drank in the romance.

And the dreams persisted after the lights had gone up and they had gone back to their attic bedrooms. The dreams were a way of escape from the monotony of their daily routine. Servant girls, like mill girls, shop girls and office girls, fell madly in love with their screen idols, and dreamed of being 'spotted' by some talent scout and being whisked off to Hollywood.

'You go the pictures last night, Maggie?'

'Aye,' said Maggie, 'aw lass, it wor luvly! Ronald Coleman! an' it wor a tale, just like ar Bessie an' Jim. She got turned out in't snaw, all for luv . . .'

'You go wi' a fella?' asked Tilda.

'Aye,' said Maggie, 'went wi' that new errand lad thru Fletcher's. 'Ad to pay me own fourpence an' all. He said he'd give it us inside.'

'An' didn't he?' asked Tilda.

'Naw,' said Maggie, 'I got me 'and in 'is briches pocket to get it out mesen!' – she half covered her mouth with her hand.

'*Ooh*!' squealed Tilda. 'What did he do?'

'He said "Stop it off Simmons, or I'll get yer dahn an' bite yer belly!".. .'

'Did 'e walk yer 'ome?' asked Tilda.

'Oh, aye,' said Maggie, 'up Station Road, and in that ginnil at back of Co-op, 'e romanticked me.'

'Yer *what*?' said Tilda.

'Aw, yer *knaw*!' said Maggie, 'bent reet back, like Ronald Coleman does it in't pictures. . .'

This snippet of conversation between two maids, toiling over the weekly wash in a middle class North Country house, was contributed by Mrs Woolven, in a letter from Newport, Monmouthshire. She was Tilda, the maid-of-all-work in 1929–30. Maggie was a girl who came in once a week to help with the washing. Apart from the weekly afternoon off, these girls had no freedom to do as they pleased, except in the larger households when families went away for quite long periods, leaving the staff on 'board wages', and even then they were usually under the supervision of an upper servant. In the house at Cambridge Gate where Doris Hazell worked in the 1930s, the housemaids, under parlourmaid, kitchen maid and tweeny, had the run of the house for three months every year while the family went to their house in the country.

She writes: 'The head housemaid was the only upper servant left in town. The rest of us were all young girls and when she had her half day off we got up to some merry games. I used to love trying to pick out tunes on the great organ in the front hall. I'd pedal away like mad to get plenty of air and pull out all the stops in turn, only wishing they had left the grand piano in the drawing room unlocked – but they never did.

'The under housemaid used to have a passion for sliding down the banisters from top to bottom and the kitchen maid used to dish up some weird concoctions for supper – most of them tasted pretty foul.

'But it wasn't *all* fun. We had been left behind to spring clean the house from top to bottom and we used to have a really lazy time in the first month, and then work like demons afterwards to get all the work done in time.'

Until the declining years of domestic service no paid holidays were given. Holidays abroad were for the wealthier upper classes – and the few personal servants they chose to take with them. Since the turn of the twentieth century holidays by the sea at home had become a regular part of life for the lower middle classes and a large section of the working class, particularly in the North. Millworkers from Lancashire flocked to Blackpool during 'Wakes weeks' and Londoners packed the piers and beaches at Brighton, Margate and Southend. Middle class families who rented houses at the coast during the summer quite often took the maids with them and they joined in the picnics and other outings, although they were still expected to do all the chores.

Day trips to the seaside by coach or on railway 'cheap day excursions' were of little benefit to the girls in service because they always had to be back by nine or ten o'clock from their days out. Late nights were not permitted. Neither was smoking, a habit increasingly common among young girls who worked in factories or shops.

The advent of the 'Brownie box' camera and cheap processes of developing and printing snapshots brought a great deal of pleasure into working class lives, including those of servants. Most families kept an album of photographs to be brought out on winter evenings.

Domestic servants missed home life the most at Christmas, the time when most families gathered together. They were tied to the 'family' of which they were part, but did not belong, and the work-load connected with the parties and Christmas fare was much heavier than usual. Not that they were kept in the kitchen and never allowed to join in any of the festivities, but 'Christmas in service' varied so widely from home to home that it is worth giving some reminiscences of it to show the different experiences of servants.

Servants in the great houses were usually lavishly treated at Christmas, sitting down to tables laden with fare that would have made their families at home gape in wonder. Frederick Gorst, in *Of Carriages and Kings*, describes these junketings in great detail. At Carden Park, where he was first in service as a young footman at the turn of the century, the day started in the Great Hall at eleven o'clock on Christmas morning with prayers conducted by the Squire. Afterwards the servants filed before the squire and his wife and were each presented with a golden sovereign and wished a 'Merry Christmas'.

All the staff, outdoors as well as indoors, sat down to a vast Christmas dinner in the servants' hall, decorated with boughs of evergreen and holly. From a hook in the fireplace hung a huge kettle – about four feet in diameter – filled with hot beer to which nutmeg, Jamaican ginger, cloves and cinnamon sticks were constantly added. Everyone's horn was kept filled.

Dinner was served at four long tables and wooden benches – starting with a hog's head stuffed with sausage meat and *pâté de foie gras* from the squire's own geese, with a shiny red apple in its mouth, followed by cold meats and joints of beef with Yorkshire pudding, and ending with a plum pudding, flaming with brandy.

Mr Gorst adds: 'The feast lasted for most of the afternoon and by the time everyone had left the servants' hall of the Manor House, Mr Ling [the butler] and I were almost too tired to serve Christmas dinner for the family and their guests.'

Later, in the service of the Duke of Portland at Welbeck Abbey, he was treated on an even grander scale at Christmas time. He and the other Royal footmen were given their Christmas boxes – each receiving a crisp, white old-fashioned 'fiver' in an envelope sealed with wax bearing the Portland family crest. After working hard over Christmas, the servants were given their own ball on Twelfth Night. It was held in the underground ballroom and the three great reception rooms. The skylights in the lawns above were slightly opened and there were arbours of potted palms, ferns and flowering plants.

Mr Gorst goes on: 'The rooms were beautifully decorated, just as though the Duke and Duchess were giving a ball for themselves. An orchestra from London had been engaged and a swarm of fifty waiters arrived because none of us was required to perform any duties that evening – this was the social event of *our* season.'

There were twelve hundred guests including all the staff, the tenants on the estate and their families and the tradesmen from Worksop and their wives. Says Mr Gorst, 'It was quite a revelation to see all the members of the staff in ball dress. Even the prim head housemaid looked quite chic in a velvet gown, and the head housekeeper, who wore a low-cut blue satin gown, was almost unrecognizable without her stiff, black silk dress and her belt of jangling keys. . . .

'I found that we had acquired a new kind of individuality and gaiety for the evening, and, stranger still, that we were all seeing each other from a new aspect – as people, not as servants.'

The duchess, dazzling in an ecru satin gown embroidered with pearls, with a ruby and diamond crescent in her hair and matching pendant ruby earrings, opened the ball by dancing with the steward, but she and the Duke left the ball after the first hour or two so that the atmosphere could become more relaxed. The following morning they left for a week to visit friends, to allow the excitement of champagne and dancing to fade and the established domestic routine of the ducal home to return to normal. *Noblesse oblige!*

The two Christmases described by Mr Gorst were in the English tradition of festivities shared by the family and servants. Half a

147

century earlier, an anonymous author in *The Christmas Tree* (an annual of 1857) described Christmas in a much more modest household than Welbeck Abbey: 'We had been merry all day and as soon as the lights were brought in at tea time, we came trooping into the parlour from all parts of the house -- some from the dairy, where Mary had been making butter; others from the nursery, where they had been playing at soldiers; and the rest from the apple store over the stable and the school-room, then used only as a play room, it being holiday time.

'We were all assembled in the parlour, and, after tea, my mother told us that we might have a game of romps. We needed no second bidding, and so to play we went in good earnest. We played at Hunt the Slipper and Forfeits, and I don't know how many other games, till we were called into the kitchen for a dance. A good old country dance it was, in which the family, servants and all joined, noisily enough – all but my mother, who sat under a sort of arbour of holly and other green leaves – for there were always plenty of green leaves and red berries to be got in the garden and orchard, however severe the winter might be – and encouraged us with kind words and beaming smiles.

'After we were tired of dancing – which was not soon, I assure you – a great china bowl of raisins was brought in by John the butler who acted occasionally as gardener and coachman as well, and was, in fact, a sort of Jack-of-all-trades. What fun there was, to be sure, as we ran dancing and singing round the lighted bowl, snatching the plums from the blue flames of the burning spirit, till they were all gone and the blue flames burned themselves out. Well, Snap-dragon over, we had kisses under the Mistletoe; and I recollect quite well how we all laughed when Papa took Betty the cook under the white-berried bough and gave her a great loud kiss. But our fun was not yet ended. At a signal from my mother we followed her into the dining room on the other side of the passage.

'Here a sight awaited us that surprised us one and all. The room was brightly lighted up with wax candles on sconces from the walls; and on a table in the centre there was placed a great Christmas Tree, hung all over with little lamps and bon-bons and toys and sweetmeats and bags of cakes. It was the first tree of the kind that I and my companions had ever seen – it was quite a new fashion the Christmas Tree; and my brother Tom, who had just come home from Germany, had superintended its getting up and decoration.'

The Christmas tree was popularized in England by Queen Victoria's husband Prince Albert, and the Christmas card, costing one penny, appeared in 1860. But these things were confined to the upper classes. They were not for the illiterate masses, for the women and children who worked all day, and sometimes all night, in the mills and mines, or the labourers on the land who earned only seven shillings a week. There were no Christmas holidays for *them*, so servants living in comfortable homes were indeed the most favoured members of the working classes.

Memories of Christmas in service in the twentieth century tend to be mixed, and tinged with not a little bitterness. The demands of servants had grown and not only in relation to wages and time-off. There was growing resentment at being expected to take the crumbs left over from 'upstairs', and this feeling seems to have been heightened at Christmas time. In *Below Stairs*, Margaret Powell remembers filing into the dining room on a Christmas morning in the 1920s 'Where all the family were assembled complete with Christmas smiles and social-welfare expressions. The children looked at us as though we were beings from another world.'

In this house all the servants were handed a Christmas present from the tree by the children and an envelope from the master. The envelope contained money and the presents were 'something useful', such as print dress lengths, aprons or black woollen stockings. 'Why,' asks Mrs Powell, 'did we always have to have sensible things? I think the reason they used to give us uniforms was because they knew we couldn't buy them out of our measly wages. Besides, if we were to have perfume or silk we would go astray.'

But she was better off than the servants in the house of a leading citizen of Southampton in the early 1900s recalled by his daughter Mrs Edith Melville-Steele, in a letter to the author from Tenerife: 'No leave was given on Christmas Day but as an enormous privilege the maids were invited into the drawing room to watch our parlour games. Not to take part, of course! I can visualize them now, sitting on two upright chairs, and looking completely embarrassed.'

Doris Hazel recalls that at Christmas time in the 1930s at Cambridge Gate the servants all had a present from her ladyship and a gift of money from her husband – 'The funny thing was though, that they were exactly the same every year. I always got a beautiful silk scarf and a ten shilling note, the under housemaid always had a pair of black kid gloves and the parlourmaid a brown leather handbag. They were all of excellent quality and always bought at Pemberthy's in Oxford Street. . . .'

It is an after Christmas 'treat' that stands out in her memories of the 1930s. Her employers hired a box for the servants at the pantomime at Drury Lane and the young tweeny from the East End had never been inside a theatre before. Although she had to stand at the back – the seats at the front were all taken by the 'upper servants' – it was like entering fairyland for her. She stood on tip-toe and craned her neck throughout the performance to make sure she didn't miss a single move on the stage below.

Employers were not normally in the habit of sharing pleasures with their domestics, as we have seen, but at Christmas time some of them, at least, made an exception.

12

THE SERVANT PROBLEM

*Sir, it is almost impossible to get a domestic servant in this town
and it is certainly high time this dole business ceased. The streets
are full of girls dressed to death, who frankly say that as long as
they are paid to do nothing they will continue as they are. (Letter
from a reader in Worthing, in the* Daily Mail, *April, 1923.)*

After the Great War of 1914–18 Mr Lloyd George and his Cabinet
were gripped by the fear of a revolution and imagined they were in
imminent danger of being shot by rioting mobs – fears that were
shared in most upper class clubs and drawing rooms. In Europe
empires were falling, in Ireland the Irish Republican Army was
gunning down policemen, while at home the police had been on
strike. So the fact that middle class ladies in Worthing and elsewhere were finding it impossible to recruit 'cook-generals' seems
in retrospect to be a fairly minor matter of concern.

And yet in the midst of moving troops, machine guns and even
tanks into Glasgow and concentrating another 'occupation force'
in Liverpool (three battalions of troops, a battleship and two
destroyers standing by in the Mersey), the Government took the
servant problem very seriously. It may be that the reluctance of
pre-war servants who had been drafted into factories to make
munitions, or had driven trams or worked the land during the war,
to return to their posts in the kitchens was seen as yet another
ominous sign of the general collapse of the forces of law and order.
There was a class war going on, and as Thomas Jones, the Deputy
Secretary of the Cabinet, relates in his detailed minutes of the
proceedings behind closed doors in the Cabinet Room at No. 10
Downing Street, '. . . Bonar Law so often referred to the stockbrokers as a loyal and fighting class [sic] until one felt that potential
battalions of stockbrokers were to be found in every town.'

As soon as the slaughter in Flanders was over, Sir Auckland Geddes, Minister of Reconstruction, asked a committee of ladies to look into the effects of women being employed on war work on the domestic service situation. In 1919 the Women's Advisory Committee reported to the Minister and their report (the Report on the Domestic Service Problem [Ministry of Reconstruction]) was presented to Parliament. It was the first time that the servant problem had been elevated to the status of warranting a Government inquiry.

The committee was rent by internal dissensions, reflecting the general mood of the country, but it was obvious to all the members of it that, in their own words, although the reduction in numbers of girls in service might partly be due to the war 'there was amongst girls a growing distaste for domestic service under its present conditions, and a reluctance on the part of parents to allow them to take up such work.'

The opinion of the committee was that the servant problem was mainly caused by lack of adequate training facilities: 'As a result the occupation is mainly carried on by unskilled workers who are unable on the one hand, to command for themselves satisfactory conditions of employment or, on the other, to fulfil their tasks efficiently.

'We regard the position as the more serious in that the best use is not being made of an occupation which might under other conditions provide a means of livelihood attractive to, and most suitable for, a large section of the women workers of the nation.'

The committee called for the establishment of training centres and clubs under the direction of local joint committees of workers and employers. The report suggested this 'might eventually lead to the organization of this occupation on Trade Union lines throughout the country.'

But the idea of shop stewards in the kitchen was repugnant to some of the ladies who had helped to draw up the report. The Marchioness of Londonderry, who regretted that 'pressures of work' had prevented her from attending meetings *in person*, did not feel able to sign the section on organization and conditions because she felt that many of its recommendations would 'interfere unduly in the individual character of relations between employers and workers' and widen still further the breach that already existed. She added in a letter: 'I regard any possibility of the introduction into the conditions of domestic service of the type of relations now obtainable between employers and workers in industrial life as extremely undesirable and liable to react in a disastrous manner on the whole foundation of home life.'

Another committee member, Lady Birchenough, in a memorandum, declared that servants in what they called 'better service' would greatly resent interference by outside regulations and trades union methods 'so inappropriate to their circumstances and themselves.' But she was all in favour of social clubs and discussions between servants and their employers – a plan she had always followed in a small way in her own household before introducing any changes of work or conditions.

But what was dangerously radical to some members of the committee was merely anodyne to others. Dr Marion Phillips refused to sign the report because it had failed to make any definite recommendations about wages and hours. She said in *her* memorandum: 'I believe that the reason why it is difficult to get servants today is not lack of training, but because servants are dissatisfied with the wages and hours of work. They are also dissatisfied with many matters which may roughly be classified as questions of social status, but hours and wages are fundamental.'

As we saw in Chapter 10, three members of the sub-committee on organization and conditions *had*, in fact, drawn up a detailed pay scale covering all ranks in the servant hierarchy and proposed overtime payments, with the comment: 'We realize that this is a revolutionary proposal, but make it with the object of drawing the employers' attention to the necessity of so organizing their households that maids will not, as at present, spend hours on duty on the off-chance of visitors calling, or be employed in the cleaning of useless "brights". This we know to be one of the greatest grievances domestic workers have.' Their 'revolutionary' proposal was *not* adopted.

But the sub-committee did suggest a substantial reduction in the servant's working day, fixed meal times of half an hour for breakfast, an hour for dinner and half an hour for tea, a half day off every Sunday and one afternoon and evening each week. They also suggested that free time should be allowed (not less than two hours every day) during which a servant should not be called upon to answer bells, nor do any other work, and should be free to go out or stay in.

Their other proposals included a fortnight's holiday a year on 'board wages', a night's rest of at least nine hours for young girls in service, and that employers should pay for uniforms – 'perhaps simply an overall. We think in many instances employers will agree to dispense with caps.'

Young girls and those who had been in their situations for a long time might be called by their christian names 'but this style of address ought not to be considered as a matter of course.'

Food should be of good quality, sufficient and reasonably varied 'but not necessarily the same as that provided for the employer's family, as differences of taste and habits must be allowed for.'

Written references should be compulsory and restricted to definite statements 'and should deal as little as possible with matters of opinion.'

All this was quite revolutionary enough for employers who were not used to being told by committees, however exalted, how to treat their servants. But the ladies of the committee did not mince their words: 'We are convinced that much of the dissatisfaction and discomfort felt by workers and employers arises from preventable waste of labour and bad general conditions which could be remedied. Domestic workers will not take pleasure in their work as long as much of it consists in constantly carrying by hand for unnecessary distances, often up and down stairs, considerable weights of water, food and fuel, of tending heating and cooking apparatus wasteful of labour, and of the larger cleaning processes which could be better effected by outside workers furnished with mechanical appliances. . . .

'The fact cannot be denied that domestic workers are regarded by other workers as belonging to a lower social status . . . the hours of duty compare unfavourably with that of any other occupation . . . The custom of addressing domestic workers by their christian name or surname is one of the causes of the superior attitude adopted by workers recruited from the same or even a lower social status . . . the distinctive dress which they are required to wear marks them out as a class apart, the cap being generally resented . . . Further, the attitude adopted by the Press and the stage is usually an unfortunate one, as servants are frequently represented as comic or flippant characters, and are held up to ridicule . . .'

Even the word servant, it seemed, was out of favour. 'Domestic worker' was the phrase in the revolution below stairs.

From the employers' point of view, according to the report, domestic servants now commanded the market, were in desperately short supply and were becoming increasingly unreliable. They found situations easy to get, and easy to leave. In the case of cooks and housekeepers, lack of adaptability and willingness to interchange were noted, even though high wages and high prices were forcing employers to cut down the size of their domestic staff – 'We believe that the domestic difficulty has long been felt by a large proportion of mothers as an excessive strain on their vitality, and a cause of burdensome anxiety and weariness, both of body and spirit. The trouble is none the less real that it is commonly regarded as ignoble and laughable.'

But the sub-committee on training criticized the 'unsatisfactory nature of the instruction [to servants] given by many mistresses, owing to their own ignorance of, and lack of system in, domestic matters.' They wanted the state or the local education authorities to set up domestic service schools in the same category as junior technical schools. Girls would be trained for service between the ages of fourteen and sixteen in these schools, spending two-thirds of their time on domestic subjects, and a third on general education, including elementary hygiene and the care of the body – 'Many of the committee considered that some instruction in sex hygiene was essential. The committee were unanimous in agreeing that, if undertaken, the instruction should be given by a medical woman.'

The committee also attached importance to the courses including physical exercises and organized games and the encouragement of a corporate identity, the establishment of Old Girls' Associations and so on. It was even suggested during the inquiry that a body like the Corps of Commissionaires (which placed old soldiers in jobs as doorkeepers and lift men, wearing bemedalled uniforms) should be set up to recruit women who had served in the WRNS, WAAC, WRAF or Land Army during the war – and 'desired to perpetuate Service traditions' – for domestic service.

Another idea was that hostels belonging to the Admiralty, the War Office, the Air Department and the Munitions Department could, now they were no longer required, do service as training bases for domestics.

In the way of all committees, this one spawned all manner of 'solutions', some practicable, some not. One lady prophetically proposed a system of day workers, living out, and paid an adequate wage.

Mrs Rosalind Nash was afraid that some middle class families on small incomes would not be able to afford higher wages for servants (in this, of course, she was quite correct) and warned: 'Young intellectuals will not marry if the wife's only prospect is the choice between incessant drudgery and a neglected home.' Miss Clementina Black suggested that these families should get together and form groups to 'establish a common centre for buying, preparing and distributing food and for providing central heating and hot water. . . .'

It sounded not unlike Communism – the Red revolution was everywhere!

But the committee had investigated the servant problem with commendable thoroughness and put its finger on many of the root causes of the crisis. As far as the recommendations were concerned, the Government looked at them and put the report in a pigeon-hole. And as far as we can tell, little or no action was taken to implement it. Governments are fond of setting up inquiries, even if they rarely do anything about the findings.

However, some efforts were made in the years immediately after the 1914–18 war to coax, even coerce, women back into 'service' and to find new recruits from the ranks of the unemployed. The Government even provided free uniforms for those who were willing to take jobs as living-in domestic servants but had no suitable clothes or the money to buy them. The Central Committee on Women's Training and Employment said in its report to the Minister of Labour in 1923–24 that 3837 women had been kitted out as servants at a total cost to the British taxpayer of £12,470. The committee had been set up originally to recruit women for war work. It was reappointed in 1920 to deal with post-war unemployment among women, with a grant from the National Relief Fund and also ran 'homecraft' and 'home-maker' courses. By the end of 1924 it had sent 25,000 women on these courses at a cost of £400,000.

But there was a snag to the homecraft course, as far as many unemployed women were concerned – they had to give an undertaking that at the end of the course, during which they were paid a 'maintenance allowance' of £1 per week, they would enter resident domestic service. This undertaking was imposed at the insistence of the Minister of Labour in 1921. Women with a regular trade to which they expected to return when employment improved, refused to sign, and the committee and many women's organizations continually urged the Government to drop the undertaking and try to find openings other than domestic service for which unemployed women might be trained – midwifery, nursing, comptometer operating, shorthand and typing were mentioned as alternatives.

The pledge to go into service was not required on 'home-maker' courses, although the training was similar and designed to 'counteract the demoralizing effects of unemployment among women.' Considerable sums were being spent on relief work for men, but England was far from being the 'land fit for heroes to live in' that Lloyd George had promised it would be when the Great War was over. Eventually, in January, 1924, the Minister of Labour agreed to remove the undertaking to enter resident domestic service and the two courses for women became one, known simply as the 'home training course'.

As the daily flood of angry letters to papers like the *Daily Mail* showed, a large section of middle class opinion considered it to be no more than the Government's duty to restore supplies of domestic labour for private households. They believed that while there were vacancies in domestic service, *no* women should receive unemployment benefit. They wanted, in short, a system of forced labour.

There was little or no support for such a notion in Government circles, but women who had been in service before the war were told by local employment exchanges that they were not covered by the unemployment insurance scheme and not entitled to draw the 'dole'. If employers who knew these girls reported to the authorities that Miss So-and-so had been in service before the war, her benefit was stopped immediately. 'After the war I refused to go back into service, to the indignation of the tribunal which refused to register us for other jobs and tried to keep our money back. I was drawing £1 a week unemployment benefit, for which I had paid in during the war while on factory work. I won in the end, and worked in my uncle's garage until I got married.' (Lily Graham, in a letter to the author from Alton, Hants.)

In 1923 another Government inquiry was set up to investigate the shortage of female domestic labour and particularly to see what effect the unemployment benefits scheme had in this connection.

The chairman was Mrs Ethel M. Wood and the committee was in session for sixteen full days and two half days, taking evidence from a large number of witnesses. It duly reported to the Minister of Labour, Sir Montague Barlow, who had appointed it. (*Report on the Supply of Female Domestic Servants*. [Ministry of Labour, 1923])

The witnesses included Countess Bathurst, for employers, Lady Cuncliffe of the Girls' Friendly Society, Miss Massey from Masseys Servants' Agency, and Councillor Jessie Stephen – one of the three who drew up the 'revolutionary' wages plan in the previous committee – representing the Domestic Servants' and Hotel Workers' Union.

The prevailing mood when the committee sat can be judged from the newspapers. The *Daily Mail*, under the heading 'Scandals of the Dole', published letters like the one we quoted at the beginning of this chapter or the ones signed by 'A Middle Class Mother, Hitchen' and a colonel at Bournemouth, claiming that girls would not take service because they could get 'something for nothing' from the state, and calling it a 'crying shame' and a 'disgrace'. A lady at Chester said she had had to give up curing her own bacon, and was thinking of giving up her dairy and poultry, because she could not get an experienced cook. They complained that they were doing everything for their maids' comfort – giving high salaries, providing every labour-saving device, short hours, even 'wireless concerts' – but girls would not work.

At the same time the more left-wing *Daily Herald* was publishing case histories of girls who had had their dole stopped because they would not 'take service': 'Miss Clift, a fragile girl, pale-faced with great dark eyes, who lost a clerical job after five and a half years, with a widowed mother whom she has to keep. "I told the exchange I wasn't healthy enough to take on domestic service", she explained. She is now waiting to hear that her dole has been stopped. . . .'

The committee investigated the complaints and found it a very unprofitable exercise. In some cases the correspondents were untraceable, their stories failed to stand up and they were unable to produce any factual evidence to substantiate their sweeping contentions.

Mrs Hughes, of West Kensington, had written a letter to the *Daily Mail* (21 April 1923) which said: 'Although my house has no basement, and there are gas fires in every room and only two people in the family, I could not get a girl at the Labour Exchange although I offered £40 a year and treatment like one of the family. At the other end of the counter stood a long line of girls, all waiting to draw the dole. There ought not to be a single healthy young woman drawing the dole and living in idleness upon the unfortunate taxpayer.' Upon investigating at the local employment exchanges, the committee could find no trace of any order having been received from a Mrs Hughes.

Even evidence submitted by a London County Council School Care Committee turned out to be based more on prejudice than facts. They reported: 'Whole family TB; father and mother dead and brother dying. Girl herself and her sister TB, and living with an old grandmother. On leaving school applicant was certified as fit and the doctor advised that she should go into service, and a place was offered her, but the grandmother refused. The girl went into a millinery workroom but has been out of work for months and draws unemployment pay.' But the Ministry of Labour told the committee that the girl had only just become sixteen, had never had an employment book and had never applied for, or received, unemployment benefit.

A social stigma now surrounded the job of servant: 'skivvy' and 'slavey' were commonly used by other members of the working class to describe the occupation. Girls who had taken jobs in domestic service, and felt themselves objects of ridicule and derision in the newspapers as a result, gave evidence to committee: 'I don't believe any girl minds the work. They *do* mind being ridiculed. I have suffered untold misery by the name "only a servant". Invitations out start: "Be sure and don't let it be known you are a domestic. We shouldn't like our friends to mix with servants." It's the snobbery of our own class.' (A parlourmaid.)

'Domestic service will not come into its own again until the insults and ridicule of the daily papers are stopped. Servants themselves do not consider the work degrading.' (A servant of 30–40 years' experience.)

The committee commented in its report: 'The constant caricaturing of maidservants as dirty, harassed, impertinent and somewhat grotesque creatures, and the use of contemptuous terms such as skivvy and slavey are significant. During the progress of our inquiry several most offensive and unjust articles and letters about domestic workers appeared in print, and were not only tolerated but acclaimed in some quarters . . . unfortunately these attacks and witticisms are keenly felt and resented by the girls, many of whom are young, and sensitive, as the young usually are, to ridicule however ill-founded. . . . The reference by a witness to the domestic worker's lack of opportunity for cultivating a talent for music aroused only ridicule and sarcasm in the daily press.'

The question of the servant's status – or lack of it – in society dominated this report, with references to it in almost every section – 'What is the good of preaching about it being a dignified calling if they are treated as undignified beings? A domestic servant is deliberately made to feel that she is inferior to anyone else.' (A housekeeper.)

'Some of them [the employers] make the maids so much lower than themselves – when there is not such a big difference after all.' (A housemaid.)

The report found that domestic service had failed to keep pace with the great change in industrial life in England – fixed hours, recognized rates of pay, inspection of factories, better social and recreational facilities and many other progressive developments – and: 'Generally speaking, employers are too prone to acquiesce in the subordination of the legitimate desires and interests of domestic workers to their own convenience. It is also undoubtedly true that many people who can only afford to keep one maid expect far too much from her.'

The domestic servant's need for recreation was still so little recognized, added the report, that many employers expected their maids to take their free evenings at different times to suit the former's convenience, so that it was impossible for the girl to make plans ahead. It was noted: 'The extension of day work is difficult because of the objection of private employers to any change in their accustomed procedure.'

The committee came up with little that was new in the way of recommendations. Indeed its proposals were less far-reaching than those of its predecessor. It recommended, predictably, more labour-saving devices in the home: regular use of vacuum cleaners, elimination of open fires, installation of indoor lavatory facilities.

The members agreed with the previous committee that training was all-important. They seemed to think that if only girls could be caught young enough, in the elementary schools, and trained as maids all would be well.

Like the 1919 report, this second official pronouncement on the servant problem was consigned to the archives of State papers, where it gathered dust and was quickly forgotten. It was, after all, impossible to legislate to change employers' views of servants and

160

servants' views of employers, or the way the public saw domestic service.

Violet M. Firth, whose book *The Psychology of the Servant Problem* was published in 1925, wrote: 'The employing classes are, for the most part, well intentioned but they have no conception of what domestic service means to the servant.' Miss Firth, a psychologist, was herself middle class but during the 1914–18 war she had worked as a 'lady gardener' and 'because I was also a servant and had to come in at the back door, I got to know the minds and feelings of the girls I met during those three years in a way I could never have done had I descended upon them from an above-stairs Olympus, however democratic my intentions might have been.'

Miss Firth discovered during the war that to be a servant was painful to one's self-respect. The mistress did not demand work alone, she also demanded a certain manner from the servant, a subservience indicating outwardly the social inferiority of the girl who served. Miss Firth writes: 'The middle class women are rigorous in their enforcement of caste reverence . . . They are so habituated to the presence of a being from another sphere who is credited with a blissful freedom from human feelings that it is a shock to them to find human nature akin to their own concealed by a servant's apron.'

Servants were, after all, human. Witnessing at close quarters a social sphere in which some worked and some did not, they wished for money and leisure, too. In their dreams these girls pictured themselves being 'spotted' by some talent scout for a Hollywood movie mogul, driving in expensive cars, cruising in yachts, being pursued everywhere by the Press.

Foolish, of course, but unlike their mothers these children of the new generation did not know, or rather would not accept, their place in the order of things. Forced into service from economic necessity, they harboured a sense of resentment against the double standards which they saw all about them: elaborate food which they prepared but were not allowed to eat except as leftovers from the table upstairs, beautifully furnished rooms for the family compared with their own austere and comfortless attics, unnecessary drudgery in the kitchen because the employers resented spending money on labour-saving devices as long as they had servants to do the chores.

The employing class was at a loss to understand the 'prejudice' of young working class people against living in as servants. People who had never worked had little idea of the feelings of a woman who had been on her feet since dawn being sent on a needless errand by a woman who had done nothing but amuse herself all day. Late dinner, for instance, was seen as a necessity of life, although it meant extending the working day of the servants far into the night. In the case of a living-in maid these hours were never added up. Employers objected to the extension of domestic work on a daily basis (servants living out) because it would mean changes in their accustomed procedure. The daily servant had fixed hours and made her own conditions of life with the money she earned. Maids liked it but mistresses did not.

A shift system among domestics was seen as a possible solution to the problem of how to cover the fifteen to eighteen hour day which started at dawn with fire lighting and ended late at night or in the early hours with the ritual of hot water bottles. But of course this would cost more and was beyond the reach of most middle class incomes. As Miss Firth pointed out, in large establishments the servant was part of a well-ordered system and the subordinate, but not the inferior, of the person in charge. Servants in houses where the mistress was also the administrator were up against an unyielding social system, an entrenched viewpoint, a rigid mental attitude. The fact was that the middle classes were overburdened by the standard of living they insisted upon maintaining for themselves, a standard modelled on that of the wealthy upper classes: 'The suburban villa is a miniature mansion and the mistress of it endeavours, with the help of some ignorant little girl, to have the same ritual of front door and late dinner that is carried out with a butler and a footman. Drawing room, dining room, brass knockers and lace curtains conspire to wreck her health when she has to contend with them single-handed.'

Servants often bore the brunt of the desperate struggle of their employers to 'keep up appearances', a situation graphically described by Miss Firth: 'The woman in the fashionable silk frock tells the woman in the washed-out print dress that she cannot afford to give higher wages. In the evening the woman in the kitchen uses her scanty leisure to patch the print dress where it has given way during the day, and so make it hang together a little longer.

'Then she goes into the dining room to serve dinner and sees that the silk frock has been changed for a satin frock. Next evening she patches the print dress again because the material, never strong, is rotten with wear and washing. When she goes into the dining room she sees that the satin frock is replaced by a lace frock.'

Undoubtedly, the worst damage to the system of domestic service was done at the lower end of the scale. Too many people who could not really afford to keep servants insisted on doing so, and lowered standards of domestic service as a whole.

Jean Hunt, in a letter to the author, recalls: 'My mother and her friends were always moaning about the awful servants they got from the Registry Office. We had a thief, a drunkard, a bloody-minded swearer, a "Piccadilly Nancy" with long black hair full of nits, and a compulsive eater . . . but we also had some wonderful ones who stayed for years. When they were ill, they were nursed by my mother like one of us and they always had exactly the same food . . . I was scandalized by one school friend at the day grammar school I went to, who said that *their* maid had margarine, while they had butter . . .

'There was also a descent in how they looked. My grand-mothers' maids had morning uniforms and afternoon uniforms, and their white caps were always spotless. My mother's maids never wore caps and weren't too particular about their pinnies, though they did have clean ones to answer the door in the afternoon and evening. Gradually, they were always out in the evenings.

'In the late 1920s and the 1930s, my mother did practically all the cooking, but the little maid did the cleaning and took the baby out in the afternoons. As we grew older one of us would answer the door, and we always did our own chores like bed-making and shoe-cleaning. My mother's last-ever maid left in 1942 to "make screws and bolts" in a war-time factory. . . .'

The Great War had left breaches in the rigid barriers that divided the social classes in England. But in peacetime there was a tendency for the *status quo* to be restored. Employers hankered for the old ways, insisting on the old deferences being shown. For example, one of the author's correspondents, an Army major who started his working life as a hall boy in a large country house in 1930, remembers that the duty he most disliked was that required of him when her ladyship went for a drive in her Rolls-Royce. He had to wear a cloth cap and walk a quarter of a mile to the park gate, which was kept closed. As the Rolls swept down the long gravel drive, it was his duty to open the gate, and as the car drew level with him, to doff the cloth cap. This performance had to be repeated when the lady of the house returned.

Servants remained near the bottom of the social ladder. Only the unemployed or criminals, down-and-outs or prostitutes were lower. Even though women over thirty were granted the franchise in 1918, the mass of women servants were without the vote until 1928, when the age limit was lowered to twenty-one. They were not, in any case, a politically-conscious class. If they had any politics at all, they could usually be expected to follow the politics of their employers – Conservative. The growth of the working class movement passed them by. Attempts were made to form trades unions of servants as long ago as 1872 in Dundee and Leamington, and the London and Provincial Domestic Servants' Union was founded early in the 1890s but never attracted a large membership. There was also a domestic section of the Workers' Union and the Domestic Servants' and Hotel Workers' Union. None of them achieved anything worth remembering in improving below stairs' conditions.

Mrs Savilla Connolly wrote to the author from North-west London: 'In 1938 some friends and I worked hard to get a Domestic Workers' Union going. We canvassed houses in the Primrose Hill and St John's Wood areas (they nearly all had servants then). We had just held an inaugural meeting at Transport House and got official recognition when the Second World War broke out and we all drifted apart.' In sheer numbers domestic servants could have formed a powerful union, but they were scattered, had difficulty in attending meetings and were sensitive to pressures from 'upstairs'.

Census figures show that the decline in the numbers of servants started after 1891 when there were nearly one and a half million men and women, boys and girls, employed in private households, but the downward trend was gradual. In 1911, the numbers were over 1,300,000, and in 1921 they were down to 1,232,046 – a decrease, in fact, of nearly 82,000, while those in the middle classes, who wanted to employ servants, were increasing all the time.

The servant problem of the twenties and thirties was not new. There had always been a servant problem: Jonathan Swift wrote about it in the eighteenth century and mention of it occurs in Thomas More's *Utopia*. The difference in the period following the

First World War was that it had become a national crisis. The war had widened the job opportunities available to working class women and they found definite hours and a measure of independence more to their liking than the wretched conditions of many places 'in service'. The spread of education, popular journalism, films and radio all opened new horizons for the working classes and contributed to their reluctance to work as servants.

But for all the changes in social attitudes, there was no open rebellion among the domestic servant class. The main factor that arrested, and even temporarily reversed, the decline in the supply of servants was the high unemployment and severe economic hardship experienced between the wars. Work in somebody else's kitchen was better than no work at all.

The 1931 Census returns show a total of 1,332,224 women (73,789 of them girls of fourteen or fifteen years of age) and 78,489 men in private domestic service. So the total was almost, although not quite, back to the peak level of the 1890s. This marked the sunset of the Great Age of Servants.

In 1931 a Bill was introduced into Parliament to do something at last about improving conditions by setting up a Domestic Service Commission under the Ministry of Labour. The Commission's duties were to include reviewing conditions of employment and wages and to draw up a servants' Charter covering working conditions, hours, wages, holidays, accommodation and recreation. All these proposed changes were well-intentioned but they never came to anything. By the early 1930s the domestic servant was still not covered by unemployment insurance, there was still no minimum wage or limit on the number of hours that should be worked, no way of inspecting servants' living quarters or ensuring that they were given enough to eat.

The Government's lethargy when it came to taking action is partly explained by the absence of pressure from any organized group. The servants, as we have seen, never managed to form themselves into an effective union. Employers on the whole were reluctant to change their own habits to meet the legitimate desires of their servants. The mistress wanted a maid who was entirely at her disposal except for certain afternoons off. She did not want a person who was at her own disposal except for specified daily hours of duty. The drawbacks to living in as a servant were the long and indefinite hours, the restricted opportunities for leisure and social life, class distinction and lack of home life.

State education was not geared to producing servants. Teachers in elementary schools in the 1920s would recommend none but the dullest girls to think of going into service. It was not surprising that the first generation of English working class children who had a chance of going to high school preferred to be secretaries rather than housekeepers or typists rather than parlourmaids. Office work was the most sought after occupation for girls, shop work came second, factory work third and domestic service a poor last resort. The girl in service had good food, good housing and £30 odd a year as pocket money. She was materially better off than the shop assistant or factory hand who had to keep herself out of her earnings. Even so, the girl who accepted this position was despised by the girl who had found a job in which she could sell her labour without selling her independence. When the shop girl had finished her (admittedly long) day she was free to do as she pleased. The maid was not. Mistresses would argue that in a private house a girl was not working all the time, but even so she was not free to leave the house.

Things were, however, changing slowly despite the employers' resistance. In the previous generation every cook had to undertake the heavy work of kneading dough for bread-making and every household had to endure the steam and tempers of wash day. In the 1920s and the 1930s bread and cakes came from the bakery and the washing went to an outside laundry. Jams and ale were bought ready-made instead of being made at home by the servants. Little restaurants sprang up all over London, relieving domestic staffs of the work of preparing late dinner. More and more household tasks were being handed over to outside specialists.

But these changes did not come about overnight. The outlook and standards of living of employers and servants were worlds apart. Mistresses tried all ways to get and keep girls in service. They gave higher wages, but that was useless – servants merely took the money and retained their grudge. The employers could not or would not see it from the servant's point of view. They were prepared to do almost anything to obtain suitable domestics except change the rules of service. Therein lay the root of the servant problem. Without a radical change in outlook, upstairs and downstairs, it was impossible to remove the stigma, the sense of personal indignity, that went with the role of servant. And that was really why the whole curious order finally collapsed and died.

Many people were antagonistic towards domestic service after the Second World War, as after the First. But the social changes of the Second World War were of much greater magnitude. In 1945, popular feeling against privilege and 'class' was expressed in the landslide victory of the Labour Government. There would be no place for 'skivvies' or 'slavies' in the new Jerusalem. In the long run, however, the economic levelling of the population was probably of greater significance in removing class distinction and the idea of 'knowing one's place'.

Two great wars and the fluctuation of commerce that went with them, made poor men rich and rich men poor. The respect accorded to breeding would not be given to the new rich. Death duties and taxes eroded the private fortunes of the landed gentry, while in the second half of the twentieth century working class affluence grew.

There is a great deal of nostalgia – among employers and former servants alike – for the Great Age of Servants. Not everything that vanished with that era was bad. Mrs G. W. Griffith of Herringham, Norwich, in a letter to the author, speaks for many when she says: 'In all the senseless clash and clamour of today when there is no peace, no standards, and apparently no aim in life, and certainly little happiness and no contentment however much people "have", one looks back with great contentment, thankfulness and happiness to a so much more worthwhile life . . . I still have regular letters from seven former maids and some living far away always come to see me when they're home in Norfolk.' And in another letter to the author, a former lady's maid in the 1920s writes: 'I don't regret my life as a general dogsbody. I had a lot of laughs once I got used to the regime and being called by my surname (an honour that). I still keep in touch with my lady, but she's nearly ninety and I'm seventy-two.'

But we can no more return to the old system of domestic service in England than we could go back to coal-fired ovens, hip baths or Wellington knife-cleaning powder. All that toil has gone for good. This book was written for those who lived at the top and worked at the bottom: the tweeny, the scullery maid, the boot boy and the butler. May they rest in peace.

Postscript

Servants, once a part of the furniture of middle- and upper-class homes, have become in our day the ultimate status symbol. Detailed tables compiled from the 1971 Census show only 32,000 servants resident in private households, less than a third of the number even ten years previously. Indeed, only three hundred households in Britain boasted three or more living-in servants.

Similar tables from the 1981 Census have yet to be published but the continued downward trend of resident domestic employment, despite the marked rise in unemployment generally over the past decade, is clear.

The select little band still 'in service' is but a remnant of the below-stairs army of a million and more that existed in Britain as recently as fifty years ago.

Of course, the official statistics take no account of people who are technically unemployed, but who earn wages in cash for domestic services – undetected by the Inland Revenue or the Department of Health and Social Security. There is reason for believing that a significant part of the black economy revolves round casual work of this sort.

But the Census does confirm the dramatic social change which has taken place in our lives with the coming of labour-saving equipment in the home and, just as significantly, the welfare state. Gone are the formidable housekeepers and rotund, flour-spattered cooks like Mrs Bridges. Gone, too, are the matronly Nannies – now replaced by fresh-cheeked young girls with college diplomas. And gone is the classic English butler like P. G. Wodehouse's Beach whose voice was like 'good port made audible'. The liveried footmen at Buckingham Palace are members of a trade union.

Even Arthur Inch, one of the last survivors of the buttling breed, has put aside his green baize apron and devotes his retirement in Sussex to the study of his own family's genealogy, though occasionally he appears on television to describe how he used to iron the pages of *The Times* for the ladies and gentlemen upstairs.

The butler in a white jacket who answers the door at a grand country house is probably not one of this breed – more likely he is newly arrived from Spain, and the housemaid upstairs may well be from Portugal or the Phillipines.

Oxford and Cambridge remain among the last bastions of the tradition of service, where a host of 'scouts' and other servants still perform the same basic menial tasks as their grandfathers did, while the young Duke of Westminster, one of Europe's richest men, still manages to employ eight full-time gamekeepers on his grouse moor at Abbeystead. These survivals from the Great Age of Servants merely emphasize its passing elsewhere.

In an interview with the author in 1973, Lady Montagu of Beaulieu remarked: 'Visiting Americans expect an English lord to have a butler and lots of servants. Most of my friends don't have them and I consider myself rather fortunate to have a staff, though it does impose certain restrictions. One has got to be on time for meals, because cook will soon give notice if you keep appearing late. Young people don't come into service these days – at least only some rather peculiar ones who think it's an easy life but soon find out that it isn't, and leave.'

By no means all aristocrats are millionaires, and many of those listed in *Burke's Landed Gentry* have to get by in a style which their fathers, let alone their grandfathers, would have considered degrading. The Marquis of Bath, quoted early on in this book, also told the author that when his living-in married couple took the weekend off 'my wife does the cooking and I go and do the washing-up. I don't mind doing it because it's only periodically. I wouldn't like to do it every day. My father would never have dreamed of washing-up. I should think he would have broken every dish he ever touched . . . he wouldn't have known how to hold one'.

That is how a peer of the realm, who came into the world in 1905 surrounded by no fewer than forty-three indoor servants alone, lives now. And of course this stark change in lifestyle can be observed lower down the social scale. At the country home of a merchant banker, for instance, one elderly butler, valet and general factotum struggles single-handedly to cope with the tasks of ten men who worked in the pantry of these large houses before the war.

The cost of keeping a full staff of, say, ten servants (butler, cook, footman, two upstairs maids, kitchen maid, four gardeners) runs well into five figures annually, to say nothing of the cost of food, accommodation, heating, lighting and so on. None but the richest can afford such domestic opulence.

Yet servants' agencies such as Massey's of Baker Street (established in 1845) and Mrs Lines in Kensington survive, although Mrs Hunt, the most famous of them all, has gone to that great Mop Fair in the sky.

Their task in meeting the insatiable demand for domestics who won't ruin the Chinese tapestry and know how to iron silk underclothes calls for infinite diplomacy and tact, since the queue of potential employers is far longer than the list of applicants. Few recruits enter resident domestic service these days because of the uncertain hours and the sometimes derisory wages.

In the old days employers specified 'no followers' when young girls applied for situations as maids. If the girl managed, despite all obstacles, to get a boy to propose marriage she left – even sooner if she became pregnant. Domestic service today, on the other hand, could not survive without the married couples and one-parent families who are attracted to it by the free board and lodging.

Employers are happy to provide a free cottage or flat with colour television and everything else, sometimes even a car, to secure the services of honest, reliable servants. Once they have found them, they try to keep quiet about it not only because such overt wealth attracts burglars but also because envious friends and acquaintances might try to entice them away.

Although domestic service remains predominantly women's work, the traditional gentleman's gentleman after the style of Jeeves still survives in Belgravia and Mayfair, but again the fortunate employer shuns publicity like the plague. As one of them explained to the author: 'Manservants are so touchy. One daren't upset them.'

According to the sociologist Dr Paul Arthyre-Clough, the servant is emerging as our newest privileged class. Out of work actors and actresses do it, violinists do it, young married couples do it, even debutante daughters do it. There is a particularly heavy demand for girls with nursery nurse certificates.

The stigma once attached to skivvying (especially in the deprived 1920s and 1930s) has disappeared along with the cap and apron. Certain Victorian values, such as knowing one's place, clearly no longer apply.

Someone in jeans or a jogging suit is now the answer to the age-old servant problem.

Acknowledgements

Wherever I have quoted directly from letters, or the interviews I conducted with many of my correspondents, these are attributed in the text, anonymously where this was necessary.

I owe especial gratitude to Mr Arthur Inch, of Haywards Heath, Sussex, who provided personal memories of his own long service as a footman and a butler, that of his father, a butler before him, and his mother, a housemaid, as well as numerous photographs and documents; to Mrs Jean Hunt, of Farnham; to Mrs Lily Graham (born 1893), of Alton, Hants.; to Doris Hazell, of Laleham, Staines; to Millicent Wardroper (born 1879); to Mr Clifton Russell Lilley, aged eighty-five, of Old Coulsdon, Surrey; to Mr C. C. Robinson, of Millom, Cumberland, a retired butler now aged ninety; to Mrs Margery Bolton, of Heysham, Lancashire, for memories of her grandmother's days of service in the 1860s; to Mrs Helen Noel-Hill, of Totnes, Devon; To Mr E. W. E. Booth FCA, FRCO, of Westbourne, Bournmouth; and to very many others, not least of all my mother, from whom I gained my earliest knowledge of the subject . . .

Apart from correspondents' letters I have drawn extensively on material from published sources, including official reports and statistics:

SOCIAL AND ECONOMIC HISTORY

The Condition of England (C. F. E. Masterman); *Life and Labour in London* (Charles Booth, 1889); *The End of an Era* (John Montgomery, 1968); *Illustrated English Social History*, Volume 4 (G. M. Trevelyan, 1942); *The Victorians* (Sir Charles Petrie, 1960); *The Other Victorians* (Stephen Marcus, 1969); *Women Workers and the Industrial Revolution* (Dr Ivy Pinchbeck, 1930); *The Making of the English Working Class* (E. P. Thompson, 1963); *What the Butler Saw* (E. S. Turner, 1962); *The Psychology of the Servant Problem* (Violet M.

172

Firth, 1925); *Salisbury, 1830–1903* (A. L. Kennedy); *The Domestic Servant Class in Eighteenth-Century England* (J. J. Hecht, 1956); *The English Abigail* (Dorothy M. Stuart, 1946); *The Rise of the Meritocracy* (Dr Michael Young, 1970); *Faithful Servants* (Arthur J. Munby, 1891); *Munby: Man of Two Worlds, The Life and Diaries of Arthur J. Munby 1828–1910* (Derek Hudson, 1972); *The Queen's Resolve* (Charles Bullock, 1901); *Seen and Not Heard* (Nigel Temple, 1970); *The Victorian Underworld* (Kellow Chesney, 1970).

MEMOIRS

Of Carriages and Kings (F. J. Gorst, 1956); *Below Stairs* (Margaret Powell, 1968); *A Picture of Life, 1872–1940* (Viscount Mersey of Toxteth); *My Secret Life* (anonymous, 1967).

NEWSPAPERS AND JOURNALS

The Times, Morning Post, Daily Mail, Daily Herald, Observer, Spectator, Contemporary Review (1910), *Primitive Methodist Magazine, Sphere, Punch, Lancet, Macmillan's Magazine* (1871).

ANNUALS

Girl's Own Annual (1896); *Every Boy's Annual* (1871); *The Christmas Tree* (1857); *Boy's Own Book* (1878).

TRACTS, PAMPHLETS AND OTHER CONTEMPORARY SOURCES

Directions to Servants (Jonathan Swift, 1745); *Serious Advice and Warning to Servants* (Thomas Broughton, 1763); *Present for a Servant Maid* (Eliza Haywood); *The Complete Servant* (Samuel and Sarah Adams, 1825); *The Servant's Friend* (Mrs Trimmer, 1824); *Family Manual and Servant's Guide* (1835); *Sermon to Domestic Servants* (Reverend George Clayton, 1840); *The Greatest Plague in Life* (H. and A. Mayhew, 1847); *A Few Rules for the Manners of Servants in Good Families* (Ladies' Sanitary Association, 1901); *Domestic Servants as They Are and as They Ought to Be* (1859); *Our Servants: Their Duties to Us and Ours to Them* (Mrs Eliot James 1883); Houlston's Industrial Library; *Home Scenes and Influences* (1866); *Original Poems* (1868); *Society Pictures from the Collection of Mr Punch* (1891) and

English Society (from *Harpers*), both being the work of George du Maurier.

HOUSEHOLD MANUALS

Spon's (1894); *The Housekeeper's Oracle* (Dr William Kitchiner); *The Footman and Butler – their duties and how to perform them* (by Williams); *Handy Book for the Young General Servant* (Mrs J. G. Baker, 1909); *Every Woman's Encyclopaedia*, Volume Two (1910); *Warne's Model Cookery* (c. 1890); *Mrs Beeton's Book of Household Management* (1861).

DRAMA AND FICTION

High Life Below Stairs (James Townley, 1775); *The Admirable Crichton* (J. M. Barrie, 1941); *Ring for Jeeves* (P. G. Wodehouse, 1963).

OFFICIAL RECORDS

Report on the Domestic Service Problem (Ministry of Reconstruction, 1919); *Report on the Supply of Female Domestic Servants* (Ministry of Labour, 1923); *Bill to establish a Domestic Service Commission 1930–31; Report to the Ministry of Labour of the Central Committee on Women's Training and Employment* (1923–24); *Bill to regulate hours of work and conditions in domestic service* (not published, 1911); official Census returns from 1871 to 1951.

I am also grateful to the staff of the British Museum Reading Room (and particularly, that of the State Paper Room) for their help in tracing source material.

Index

Books in National Trust Classics

Bath
Edith Sitwell
A lively and unorthodox look at the development of Bath
from the arrival of Beau Nash in 1702 to the end of the
century, concentrating on Bath society, written in 1932.

The Earls of Creation
James Lees-Milne
The five Earls who are the subject of this book flourished
at a time when the amateur exercised great influence
over taste. Burlington, Pembroke, Leicester, Oxford and
Bathurst created superb domains, most of which are still
standing unaltered today.

Felbrigg, The Story of a House
R. W. Ketton-Cremer
Introduction by Wilhelmine Harrod
First published in 1962, this memoir is the history of a
Norfolk country house from the seventeenth century
until the 1960s, and the four families who have lived
there. Written by one of the last members of the
Wyndham family who bequeathed the house to the
National Trust in 1969, the book pays tribute to this great
house and its traditions.

First And Last Loves
John Betjeman
Illustrations by John Piper
An exuberant, convivial and affectionate collection of
essays in which Betjeman writes very much as he was
wont to speak, considering examples of architecture

from Cheltenham to Leeds, London's railway stations to Ilfracombe's summer residences.

Ghastly Good Taste
Or, a depressing story of the Rise and Fall of English Architecture
John Betjeman
Ghastly Good Taste is Betjeman's witty and often irreverent guide to the history of architectural taste, in which he works his way through from the beauty of the Gothic period to the 'horrors' of the 1930s, with his distinctive narrative flair and gift of the unexpected evident throughout.

The Housekeeping Book of Susanna Whatman
Susanna Whatman
Introduction by Christina Hardyment
As Mistress of Turkey Court, Kent, Susanna Whatman wrote down detailed household instructions for her servants, giving a fascinating picture of life 'below stairs' in an eighteenth-century house. The introduction gives a comprehensive account of housekeeping through the ages.

In A Gloucestershire Garden
Canon Ellacombe
Introduction by Rosemary Verey
Very little now remains of the exquisite garden of Bitton Vicarage near Bristol which Canon Ellacombe created during the last half of the nineteenth century. But in a series of articles which he wrote for the *Guardian* the Canon described how, season by season, step by step, he lovingly chose, planted, pruned and shaped the shrubs, flowers and herbs which drew visitors from near and far.

These articles were collected into one volume and published as *In A Gloucestershire Garden*.

Made in England
Dorothy Hartley
First published in 1939, *Made in England* is a unique guide to some of the age-old country jobs and skills then being practised in England, portraying the often unsung accomplishments of traditional England.

The Rule of Taste
John Steegman
Introduction by Gavin Stamp
First published in 1968, Steegman's entertaining book traces the various changes in the arts of gardening, architecture and painting from the early eighteenth century to the early nineteenth century.

Rustic Adornments for Homes of Taste
Shirley Hibberd
Introduction by D. J. Sales
A guide to home improvements, published in 1856 for the prosperous new middle class of Victorian England. It gives intriguing advice on the creation of aviaries, aquariums, rockeries, ferneries, Wardian cases in which to grow plants, and such garden embellishments as grottoes and arches.

Victorian Taste
John Steegman
Foreword by Sir Nikolaus Pevsner
First published in 1980 as *Consort of Taste 1830–70*, *Victorian Taste* tackles the period covering twenty years on either

side of the Great Exhibition, and includes lively portraits of key figures.

The Wild Garden
William Robinson
Introduction by Richard Mabey
The Wild Garden, published in 1870, has had a profound influence on gardening thought and theory, and has never been more topical than today, when so much of our wayside and woodland flowers are being lost to urban development and insecticides. In it William Robinson attacks the formal artificiality of high-Victorian gardens and passionately advocates the planting of wild and native flowers. William Robinson worked in Irish gardens from boyhood until recommended to the Royal Botanic Society's garden in Regent's Park.

Gallipot Eyes
A Wiltshire Diary
Elspeth Huxley
An evocative diary of village life in a small Wiltshire community by the well-known author of *The Flame Trees of Thika*. Elspeth Huxley's diary records her everyday preoccupations, describes the people round her and notes the ever-changing patterns of existence.

Uppark and Its People
Margaret Meade-Fetherstonhaugh and Oliver Warner
Introduction by Martin Drury
An entertaining portrait of life over three centuries in the late 17th-century house of Uppark, built high on the Sussex Downs and now one of the National Trust's most highly regarded houses of its period.